THINGS (Important and Wise)

THAT

MUST (Need to and should)

BE SAID (and heard)

THINGS (Important and Wise)

THAT

MUST (Need to and should)

BE SAID (and heard)

"Learning to understand the chaos and blindness of Humanity; a point blank hack, stab, chop, and cut method of teaching ethical foundations; with compassion."

Al Kida

An American

To order additional copies of this book, contact:
Xlibris Corporation
1-888-795-4274
www.Xlibris.com
Orders@Xlibris.com
74767

Dedication

To All Human Beings everywhere, especially my Spouse, and my friends Mr. Freije and his Spouse.

ATTENTION AMERICA

I woke up this morning and found this book on my computer with a note telling me to publish it under my name and that I would receive further instructions when and if America woke up to "the message" that follows. The message and book were already in my computer with a note stating the author as the, "Beings in the spacecraft out your front deck door." So, here it is, a message from outer space for all Humans. It is even personalized into my style of speaking and contains sufficient legalese double talk to totally "disclaim" any and all assumptions and conclusions anyone else may ever make about what is written and encoded in the following expose of the Human existence. I went to the window, looked out, and did NOT see any "spacecraft" at my front door, so I opened the door and stepped out. There was an enormous and very fast "flash of bright white light," like a "flash cube" on an old camera going off like a "silver bullet." The flash dissipated in a flash, and the water on the lake became very disturbed for about 30 seconds on a perfectly still morning. The sun was bright and reflecting on the water, and there are some big fish in the water, so the laws of physics are responsible for a lot of alleged cosmic magic; trust me. Plus, I really wrote "the message" (this book). There are no angels or aliens hiding in the light, and hovering my over my shoulder telling me what to write. If they exist, they are out of sight, and I don't hear a sound other than what my brain makes. I was just warming up and setting the stage. Learning can be fun, as you shall see.

CHAPTER ONE

There is only one chapter in this verbal meteor shower of knowledge book. There is more knowledge contained in and on theses pages than you may be able to digest in twenty years (not bragging here, but fifty five years were required as training for me to learn the skill of using an arrangement of repetitive in no order string of individual vowel and consonant sounds to express myself; i.e. talk and write clearly in the American English language). I wrote this book primarily because I am sick of living in a society where "some people" (not ALL people, just "some people") use violence, guns, retarded laws in many cases, corruption in many forms, taxes, fines, fees, chemicals like napalm and agent orange (and a thousand other deadly prescription chemicals), threats, bribery, deeply rooted deception, libel, slander, arrogance, and other diverse forms of improbity as primary tools and weapons in "their competitive pursuit of the money" other people earn HONESTLY with sweat and risk of loss of life or severe bodily harm. I am not leaving this country, and I know there are millions of others in America who are equally as tired of the "some people" always interrupting the progress of all people with their alleged "constitutional democratic" new tax, new fines, and fees to "get their fair share" of the fruits of other people's slave labor wages. If people were flowers and weeds, I would be a rare Hawaiian orchid. In my flower state, I would be choked to near death by government employee weeds, the life sucked out of me at the roots, the light blocked from my leaves 99% of the time, and the rain water almost all used before it reaches my touching distance. Weeds are everywhere, seeking new places to seed. Weeds have an unproductive self serving interpretation of "freedom," i.e. "freedumb;" which is founded in jealousy of their ancient cousins, the flowers, and is marred by decades of perpetuated immaturity that was originally founded in an undesirable but inevitable genetic mutation. Human flowers need to unite against the spread of the

Humans weeds; i.e. Humans who refuse to get an education, who won't work, who steal, or who get an education and use the knowledge to steal on a large scale, or take unfair, abusive, economic or other advantage of others. "Some people" (Humans) go to great lengths to devise brainwashing schemes that replace real education. While "some people" MAY be "better at planning" certain things (the building of roads, bridges, bomb attacks on certain buildings from high in the sky, a new tax, etc.), clearly, the current planning does not include much in the way of benefits for the majority of the people that begin to compare to the benefits for the people who make the decisions that led to the current level of international political and economic chaos. When the current disaster is brought back under control (if ever) America will still look just like it did BEFORE the "crisis ON" switches were flipped by congress and the white house. I am at greater risk of being shot by the local sheriff than I am at risk of being blown up by Al Qaeda. I do keep company with a man on the terrorist watch list, who is not a threat to anyone, and I have told the "authorities" they are wasting their time and everyone's money; but they "don't think so." In our current position, (America) REFORM looks like revolution.

"Government" is largely a smaller group of people telling a much larger group of people "what the world is all about" with force that is administered through city, county, state, and federal divisions of police, the military, courts, banks, insurance companies, and other capitalists trying to create a paper trail TO your money. Attila the Hun may be dead, but his barbarian rape and pillage attitude and lifestyle lives on. Attila has earned his G.E.D. and learned how to dress for better success. Attila manages a portfolio of investments (without a license) that is mainly focused in banking, insurance, mortgage, and Wall Street related firms. Your money is the object of government "work," and Attila has a powerful lobby group who is well known in congress for having deep pockets. Controlling your behavior and fining you for stepping over the weed line has gotten out of control; the flowers are the real attraction here. We definitely need something stronger than Round Up, Weed Be Gone, and another amendment to control the powers of congress, who is the only group of the "some people" who CAN vote on the law (to give up the "power" they crave? I don't think so). Like horsepower potential from a gasoline powered engine, the majority of the people sit and wait for someone to start the engine. At the same time, "some people" with guns just walk into the scene, who know nothing about cars, and they start "inspecting" the engines, and decide to slow everything down by making the engineers add restrictor plates to the car engine (symbolic for taxes and laws), which will not allow the car to reach speeds over 200 mph when 230 mph is possible. (In other words, "the government" steals the potential of 30 mph). In the same manner, "capitalism, democracy, and socialism" have to have firm limits, ethics, morals, integrity, and honesty. In other words, a full grown male pit bull that grew up in a famous person's kennel may not be a good Alpha dog example for teen aged miniature poodles who grew up on a farm. When everything can be used against you, as in selling the problem and the cure; people need to stand up and unite against abusive capitalism. There is big tax money to be collected in selling you (the American middle class) ways to protect your privacy from other Americans and foreigners. Just because a seller has all the credentials, licenses, titles, and receipts proving the fees were paid, it does mean the seller is honest. Congress passed laws making it easier for people to gain access to your private personal information (in secret illegal nontaxable transactions) because there is a lot of tax to be collected in selling ways to protect your identity; do you get it? Create your own need to exist, become your own competition, create your own market; i.e. a computer virus to which you have the cure; or a glass repair or replacement company has a person break glass in hopes of getting the call for a repair. Or, lawmakers decide to order police officers to increase traffic stops 15% over the next three months to generate revenue for the police and government paper pushers retirement funding. Yes, every way you look, government is a corrupt force, a smoking gun. Police exist FIRST to protect government employees and tax collectors. No "god, God, or GOD" directed or ordered any man or woman to write anything, so kill the false paralyzing belief that Jesus is the real author of the U.S. constitution. Jesus did his job, he's done, he does not need to "come back."

Again, government is primarily first and foremost "a job" of creating an "avenue" paper trail between you, your money, and Human "government" employees. Taxation IS a competition, a competition where the "some people" plan all the ways to tax, fine, fee and economically control your enslavement (and mine) and make us pay for the enslavement (2 or 3 times) under the guise of "being served." For the "some people" who "process" the paperwork that leads to a check to pay the "some people" to enforce the law with guns, courts, fines, fees, and jail, the **competitive pursuit** for YOUR slave labor blood backed income is best defined as (government employees, teams of lawyers, police, judges speaking) 1. "We are in control, get out of the way." 2. "We made another decision, shut up and deal with it." 3. "We have thousands of trained bully cowboy officers with guns and the right to use them at their discretion to enforce the law." 4. "You voted the leadership into office and gave them the right to do whatever they want in the name of democracy." 5. "You are now free to pay us all the taxes, fines, interest, and fees that we want, so pay us or face the ugly consequences."

I have not invented any new words here, I am just an observer (educated in America) using pre-existing terminologies (re-arranged) to define a common position created with Human attitudes and behavior. I am fed up with the attitude and behavior of "some people" who "expect" all others to "get out of THEIR way" (everybody's streets are "THEIR" way) to the top of the heap where decisions are made (by a few people) that destroy cities, states, lives, and countries (meaning the civilians, people who are "collateral war losses," killed bystanders caught in the "battles of leaders" over time, real estate, money, religion, words, lies, and possessions; buildings, roads, utilities, natural resources, water and sea ports, bridges, air space, etc. "My way" is usually "around" any obstacles, so you are not in my way. The United States government (congress, people) passed a law in 2009 to stop the counting of dead civilians in Iraq and Afghanistan (dead civilians who died as a result of any type of U.S. or allied soldier behavior, such as the destruction of a home next door to the target house or Mosque, building, or cave, or from an overspray of fire power projectiles into the wrong crowd of Humanity at the meat market). Of course if the reverse were the case (Al Qaeda in the U.S. setting up camp), the story would be told different; and Al Qaeda would count the dead Americans civilians. America does not have a monopoly on the knowledge or understanding of GOD. Yes, we have separation of church and state, which explains why the courthouses across America are dressed up for Christmas and Easter. Religion and Politics both need a long overdue review. Free will can be used to explain most things in Human behavior.

I am sick of many (most) politicians automatically behaving as if they are the smartest people in the world and everybody "owes" them for what they do; tax, fine and fee us (majority of the people), put our great grandchildren in debt before they are born, lie to us, keep us enslaved, give our money away to people who hate us, spend our money developing ways to control people who do not see what the military political system is planning; i.e. an all out one party of a few too wealthy Totalitarians using the democracy logo to increase their already too bloody and decadent path of destruction and self glorification. I am for one party Totalitarian Democracy where the educated majority of the people make all the laws. Democracy is supposed to mean "leadership by the majority of the people."

Talk about "setting an example" for other people's children (and the world) to figure out and "learn to deal with" (**deal with** meaning barely tolerate, avoid contact with, let them have what they want even though they are not qualified to handle the responsibility, refuse to let them bring you down to their level, find a way to make them leave on their own); America's leaders have figured out how to use chaos to perpetuate fiction relative to fairness and equality, and outside of war, they can't "come up with" a stabilization plan that does not require the loss of life and mass bankruptcy. There is not a politician in America who would debate me on the subject of the IRS in my situation.

Eight premises of this deep impact word collection are 1. we all share common ancestry 2. all people are other people's children, regardless of the age of their body 3. "the government" is a group of people who use and abuse "their self defined rights" of discretion (far different "rights" than citizen's rights) in the collection of taxes, fines, fees, interest, and use of force 4. all people are not created equal in a worldly sense 5. all people do not deserve the exact same degree of respect, however, all people deserve no less than fair treatment and a guided opportunity to improve their respectability 6. the Rules for Professional Conduct for lawyers and judges in America are as close to being a FARCE and a FRAUD as words on paper can ever be 7. America must have new leadership and must reform internally; or become a broken nation 8. America is not truly a united organization of states, but a network of military and police installations that serve to protect the people who are the government FIRST, civilians are last.

I am not a terrorist, except to liars, who are threatened by truths that spill from my lips and fingertips. The form of terrorism I employ is physically harmless, and is actually a mental challenge for "some people" who are convinced they already know 100 or more times more than they like to believe they do know. I am the only person who knows what I know. The less intelligent a person is, the more they will "find wrong" with my perspective. I expect to be ignored by the people who need to face me the most; America's "leaders," the war, tax, fine, and fee people. I propose that we all co-operate with each other more than we compete. There is no reason why everyone cannot be retired by age 55 (or sooner if they utilize their abilities fully, even if they only operate at 80% capacity), if we all work to help make a new proposal a reality. Key words "We ALL work" and "reality." I am tired of working to make money to let "some people" take from me against my better judgment, and use my money to support their harassment of me; and use my money to support people who do not want to work or get an education. The "this is ours you owes us" attitude has to be stopped. The majority of the people do not "vote" on the wording in the writing of any laws, and clearly, the politicians who do vote on the laws, and write the bills; are out of touch with the people who pay the majority of the taxes, fines, fees, interest, and with the most blood and injuries. If I were Al Qaeda I would target my attack ONLY on government employees, especially congress, the IRS and the fingers and roots of the IRS, lawyers, judges, police officers, traffic court employees, and all the lazy, slothful, totally unproductive, deceptive and deceitful criminals, and other trouble makers; then I would start over with new and improved democracy. The good news for America is that I am Al Kida, not Al Qaeda, I was born in America, and I dislike violence. I do not make threats, but I get things done. I love life, and fun.

Like a limb on a tree that outgrows its space over a house, government abuse has grown to threatening levels; the majority of the people on the planet being threatened. This life could be more fun for more people more of the time, under the right leadership, which we do not have today in America (for the last several decades); or in the world. It is not my (or anyone's) job to let the people who are the government use my (our) money in ways I (we) would never use the money. All the 'good' people do is "used against them" in a court of law by "some people" who want a larger share of everyone's money through the law, i.e. including but not limited to taxes, fines, fees, licenses, permits, tickets, lotteries, assessments, and interest compounded at usury loan shark rates (IRS has a 120% rate). The world needs more wealthy people, and a lot less false commercial everything. The world needs a commercial only set of channels so the interrupting of the "entertainment" with commercials can be stopped. "Some people" have the capitalist freedom of speech right to interrupt your "entertainment" with commercials about anything; and every commercial is founded in a form of deceptive manipulation. Exceptionally rare is the commercial that tells the whole story. If commercial advertising and CEO bonuses were taken out of insurance rates, and if all insurance companies could never make more or less than 12% profit per year, everyone could afford every kind of insurance. If the majority votes to create such a law, it has to become law, in a real democracy. Then, if we took medical malpractice, Medicare fraud, and all the other traditional other everyday frauds out of insurance rates, everyone could afford to be over insured, and we could give the insurance company a raise to 15%, 18%; or 20%; provided ALL employees had equal pay increases and no "extra" bonuses for anyone. A problem some people will see here is that it is not competitive capitalism, and it has overtones of Socialism; which is one way of seeing the matter, which is also wrong. Democratically, the insurance industry will become highly regulated with simple rules of conduct, which if broken will be met with severe punishment; solitary confinement, hard labor, forced education, and counseling. Maybe utilities, medicine, insurance, public transportation including commercial airlines, road and bridge construction, and a few other "needed by all" things SHOULD be "democratically socialized" in a manner that is refined and defined by ALL people in a truly democratic manner. The Federal Reserve should and needs to be abolished, which, as many people claim to know, is "privately held" by a few families. The "world" can produce more wealthy, productive, ethical, honest people with integrity than what I see and hear these days "leading" the rest of us to a place that doesn't seem to exist, except for a few, like the children and grandchildren of the owners of the federal reserve. Face it ladies and gentlemen, medicine and insurance are not about saving lives and protecting everything from financial ruin, it is about money for the owners of the stock of the companies, and the CEO's, doctors, their lawyers and CFO's, etc. who protect and serve the "top executives" for their executive pay. Technically, as a matter of pure behavior and practice, America currently has "socialist" programs in place that cost tens or hundreds of millions of dollars annually.

Those in the legal system most certainly DO have an edge on others when it comes to using "everything you say AGAINST you," which includes pure simple truth. When you need a good liar, someone who can twist real facts into a self serving deceptive rhetoric scheme that pays big bucks for a few people for a while (until you get caught); get a lawyer. The "government" employs thousands of lawyers (to protect law makers from the word blunders of their "legislation" on paper). Legislation is based on intelligent interpretations of real facts, allegedly. Interpretations of events, cause and effect chain reactions, etc. are judgment and perception issues; i.e. six people will witness one event and odds are very good that each person will notice different things. In other words, too many of the same "types" of perceivers and judgers make too many "laws" that affect too many others in a negative way; i.e. "your freedom is limited to OUR guidelines and OUR interpretation of the situation; and WE only have to consider what WE want to consider, and (not necessarily ALL the facts) when WE make OUR decision about what is "best" for YOU and everyone. So, our decision will all come down to "do we like you, or do we not like you?" Virtually 100% of the time, the "some people" who are "the government" define their blunders with evasive, allusive descriptions of unclear actions, laws, and constitutional jurisdiction clauses that "wash their hands" of all responsibility associated with the blunders. I am sick of the claims that "we're just doing our job, and we did what we thought was the best at the time;" and "we don't have jurisdiction to see the point blank in your face FACTS that disprove our conclusions." If I were Al Qaeda instead of Al Kida, I would target on rounding up criminals, door to door in some areas, and I would inject a "new government constitution." The military will have to be on high alert during the time period of the changeover of leadership in America.

The intention here is a nonviolent switching, not a takeover. However, it is expected and anticipated that the current leaders will offer many forms of resistance that may or will include violence during the switch over. Think of the switch over as a tree trimming endeavor; the trimmings will be used for many positive uses. The police will have to be subdued, perhaps; and hopefully none will resist and "have to be" hand cuffed, sprayed, tazed, and beat.

I could not sleep or live with myself if I survived off the taxes, fines, fees, and interest other people were forced to pay into the pools of trillions of dollars that go into the many accounts used solely to support the millions of people who are the government, including buying their toilet paper. In my opinion, artistically speaking, if the United States was one man, he would be morbidly obese, have a hideous face, greasy fingers, food stained clothing, food pieces, ketchup and other condiments around his mouth and trailing down his humongous gut to his beltline and the floor around his desk. Uncle Sam has become an obsessive-compulsive, anal retentive, paranoid schizophrenic with violence as a form of expressing his demented perception and judgment. Too much of the collected taxes, fines, fees, etc. American citizens pay are wasted and given away to people who do not like America or who are criminals in America; old story, I know; people allow and make negative history repeat, I know, and so do you. In a real democracy, the majority of the people would have put a stop to such give-a way's a long time ago. Instead, our alleged intelligent leaders "budget" to give away a trillion or more of our dollars EVERY YEAR in the name of democracy without asking the rest of us. By now, admit it, face it, all money has blood stains, and we are all guilty in part for the wars and the causes of wars. I am sick of "following leaders" who baptize all of us with the blood of people we do not know or understand, and who we criticize without understanding the core of their beliefs. (I am not a member of any religious group, but I know there are beings with powers and intellects so far beyond ours that we can only begin to see the potential. Americans seem to be blind to the image America projects with our primitive Spartan pride). Stand back and look at what is on the television and satellites. We are all guilty (in a lesser sense than the actual "leaders") of the wars our taxes fund; simply because we stood by and watched as "some people" cheered while our leaders and hero's committed acts of war in our names with our money in order to try and gain political and economic control of the means people use to create work to help people live above the poverty level (for example; oil, gas, iron, gold, diamond deposits, a sea port, etc.) in

THEIR country. Some Americans seem to believe (behave as if) they have perfected a way to absolve themselves of "their sins" against the universe with or by mere "Human thinking and judging." The Earth is big enough for everyone, but we have to control our population in respect to our growth and technology.

In order to absorb the most superior results from the symbols (letters, words) in this space in time, just pretend, assume, conclude, think, judge, and KNOW that I am qualified to say what is written. Until America (and the world) can admit to what is written herein, and take action to eradicate the negative, progress will remain at low levels and the old up down cycle will repeat again. I am sadly not impressed to see lives in desperation being ground up and buried in mass graves by some group of people with religious and capitalist government motivations. All governments are capitalist to some degree, this is not the real issue.

Our existence is very special, despite all the potential dangers; however, Humans create most of their own problems. Americans have neglected to maintain strict control over the law makers, the collectors of the taxes, fines, and fees, the war makers, the police; and now the next 2-3-4-5 generations of the working class "children" of the slaves are destined to pay for the mistakes of the rich kids who rule the world today, like their rich kid great grandchildren's children will rule when they become grown up rich kids. I do not believe in hand outs except in extreme cases, but no one should be hungry, without a home, clothing, medical care, education, pleasure time, and full time employment. A huge problem with uneducated Humans is that they reproduce like some animals and become a burden for many, when no life should be a burden. Believe me, I know, each and every Human and all life is connected to the computer banks of the universe, we simply cannot hide from the Creator of the universe. The entire universe; as far as Humans will ever be able to see with the next more powerful telescope, was actually contained in one pre-programmed molecule. I know that is a huge concept, but the Creator(s) is (are) a genius times infinity squared a trillion times squared; based on Human ability to measure the intelligence of the universe and give it a number on an American scale.

It appears to me that "GOD'S holy planet," Earth; IS a molecular configuration of the magnificent kind in the run down part of the universe. All of the elements in our universe function co-operatively in manners that enable US to perceive a small portion of the greatness (love and appreciative happy emotion) of the creative forces. And look at what we Humans have done with our free will; we teach "the children" hate and pain based emotions over money and sex. Humans were supposed to have been taking care of Mother Earth, who could have lived forever, but who appears to need a new caretaker and some serious rehab. Competitive greed is a root cause of all economic and political failure for the masses, but Humans control competitive greed. Perhaps another more intelligent and efficient group of beings from afar are being called in from UFO land to take over the daily care, maintenance, and rehab of Earth while she is still alive. More than likely, in my opinion anyway, I agree with the potential of my good friend who proposes that IF (IF being the big word) "aliens" are responsible for any life on this planet, aliens are responsible for ALL the life on this planet. Further, life giving DNA like "string" materials were perhaps projected in egg like containers or set in place at various locations simultaneously around the planet by visitors from "outer space." If beings can fly to us or even find us in the universe, they are smarter than us. Clearly "they" (the potential aliens) seem to not want a confrontation. Their crafts are much faster than ours; we know that. We also know that whoever rules the air wins the war. We are supposed to know also that the only way at the time (WWII) to stop the Howard Hughes designed Japanese Zero aircraft, was with atomic bombs. The U.S. military rejected the air-craft design by Hughes as a matter of arrogance, which led to the intensity of WWII; the Japanese saw what Hughes saw in the craft; superior engineering.

It seems people have forgotten, and that young people just do not know, that the Second World War was well under way for some time before the U.S. became involved. The European conflicts were in process, and Japan had attacked China, and was winning the war. The U.S. told Japan that America's policy at the time was to not be involved in trade with any nation that was at war. Japan contended that the conflict between Japan and China was not a business issue with the U.S., whose leadership disagreed (over oil shipments in particular), so Japan bombed Pearl Harbor. Put this into perspective today relative to trade, oil, war, greed, political corruption, unemployment, poverty, crime, disease, alcohol abuses and crimes, extreme violence and animated war as a form of entertainment for children and adults, and what do we have? A society wherein 75% of the population are slaves to the tax system? A system of "Chaos" blessed economics?

This verbalized flow of Human experience and expression intends to redirect some of your thinking towards a good memory happy path you may have thought was now covered up with a Wal-Mart parking lot. Being Human is a very special existence. Trying to tell you what we have been prior to our Humanity is a story that is too long and dark to put in a book of this size and purpose. This "strange" compilation of word arrangements is "a key" to understanding another dimension of perception of our nuclear potential on the molecular level. Everything we perceive in this dimension is founded in light particles that are microscopic to us.

Life IS a complex molecular chemical soup in a process that was clearly genetically engineered by "beings" with higher and greater potentials than what Humans can begin to comprehend. I know this for a fact, so don't argue with me on this; life is just too incredible to be just an "accidental big bang explosion." Realistically, Human existence comes down to a small number of specific molecules. Period. This life is a slowed down version of a higher dimension; a "growth indicator" for potential life with negative and positive environments, a level of electro-magnetism, like in a slurry that is used to separate gold chips from gold dust; and all the impurities (oxides, nitrates, carbons, etc.). Humans do such a poor job managing the few potentials Humans have "discovered" (the work of Tesla for example) that apparently the universe will not allow Humans to gain any more new knowledge that would be abused like everything Humans already have and abuse for the profit of a few rather than the many (who are ravaged with confusion on how to make a lot of money in a short period of time with no skills, education, or foundation with solid roots and footers). Yes, knowledge can be wrongfully and negatively **over** used against many people by a few people (i.e. Hiroshima and Nagasaki, lottery management, health care, etc.), or for the good of people; as in building and maintaining a clean living environment (like we are not doing). For "some people," it is a lot easier to blow things up and kill by-standers to the conflict than talking sense to "law maker" personality type Human beings who also see every war as an opportunity to "grow the tax base." This strategy is one in which able bodied, aggressive, motivated to "do something for God and Country types" put their lives on the line to protect a tax maniac law maker government of Humans who find diplomatic ways to (allegedly) "justify" war (mass murder Manson style, only on a much larger scale, for example, the attitude that "those people are blocking MY way to the completion of my goals by living on that land where the oil is. You need to kill them so my buddies can get that oil." Manson was after music production; "you know who" was after the oil and the tax on the oil). It is the "simple knowledge" Humans can NOT see that is so devastating to Human relations; specifically, how "our knowledge of life" is used in our treatment of each other over "things." Commercial television is an insult of the worse kind (to myself and others) considering the mentality adults utilize to sell "things" to adults and children (simply pathetic displays); i.e. adults creating and speaking for animated characters that sell insurance, toilet paper, and other things. And using the television to "push" inter-racial marriage and acceptance of homosexuality as normal behavior to have on display. Good grief; and my friend's tax problem is REAL news that no one will put on the television. Solutions to all or most of our problems are right in front of us, but getting to the unknown in a conscious state is not always easy. Knowledge is a weapon, a tool, and a bargaining chip; something "to be used" by lawyers and courts to make billions of personal income "talking about" simple words and gross behaviors. Denial IS proof of fear, particularly fear of admitting the truth about poor use of personal judgment; i.e. supporting the killing of hundreds of thousands of Humans who lived in Iraq, who had NOTHING to do with the 9-11 attacks. THEN, "spin" the truth with deception in an effort to justify the murder because billions can be made by a few in selling advertising (and collecting taxes). "We" live in a free country for "some people," but not all of the people. Deception is a foundation of too much advertising. The rules of democracy do not apply to or control greed and capitalism; i.e. the belief that greed and corruption are "just the way it is in a capitalist free economy" that professes ethics, truth and integrity. (Hint: ethics, truth, integrity, and deception are not compatible terms). Knowledge can help people acquire money legally and illegally. America's legal system is next to being a circus and an all out farce. America is "evolving" according to the plan of the few people with the most money. American leaders waste more money every year than it would take to make everyone a millionaire. A problem is however, giving away millions of dollars to lazy, slothful people with no skills or education will not cleanse, heal, save, or rejuvenate Human thinking or Human societies.

If you are under age 40, this book may challenge a great deal of what you have been led to believe is true regarding ethics, integrity, honesty, and Human thinking. I am not the words you are reading, and the words that are this book are harmlessly aimed at everyone, self included. Relax. While SOME people are "terrorists" who HATE the American way of life, "terrorists" of another form have taken control of "the U.S. government and constitution." I am not a republican, a democrat, or a socialist. Some people are so brainwashed, it is ludicrous, to the brainwashed, that they are brainwashed. Brainwashing is used in place of education and "the commercial news" everyday in America, all day. Americans rarely get a glimpse of life that is not negatively affected by taxes, politicians, lawyers, frustration, hate, deception, greed, danger, fear, suspicion, mistrust, media spin, and the like. Guns in the hands of American soldiers are just as easily aimed at Americans (by the government and other "American citizens") as at anyone else. People "fear" the sound of certain words, call themselves brave, then run from people who say words that are TRUE about the "some people" who are the government (not the majority of the people). Americans are the number one killers of Americans. People who tax the masses three trillion dollars per year every year for decades and who waste 65% of everything collected ARE terrorists and criminals. I am not anti-American, I am anti-universal political corruption.

"The People" who tax the masses do so to maintain and improve their standard of living (with everyone's tax dollars; wasted money). I call these people "paranoid self deceivers." They lie to themselves and each other and everyone, i.e. professing to know the future of mankind from an American perspective. They can look around and see a world in trouble, but cannot see who is really pushing the action. Likewise "they" fear losing what they have acquired and fully support the idea of "killing anyone our government wants killed because Jesus made America." Anyone who is not a paranoid self deceiver is considered to be a threat to a paranoid self deceiver; so we have the "terrorist list," which my friend and I are both on. Paranoid self deceivers do not know they are paranoid self deceivers, which is why they accuse everyone else of being paranoid and living in an unreal world. Paranoid self deceivers want everyone to be paranoid self deceivers; i.e. believe the same lies (false foundations) as the paranoid self-deceivers. **"They want to take away our freedom" is NOT the principle reason people need to pay taxes (people pay taxes to support the system that taxes the masses in order to support the system that taxes the masses)**. Only "bad government" can "create pockets of resistance against a specific government activity," (cause and effect, government people act, people resist) such as forced taxation without representation by the government employees. Throw in ten thousand forms of corruption then chant "we're free and we're better than you" and "we" create our own terrorism. Taxing 75% of the masses (slaves) so 12% (prima donnas) can live in a state of "kingly" vanity, while the other 13% is homeless and desperate; is a terrorist leader's way of life. However, with well planned double talk education techniques and media support, anyone and everyone who opposes what some perceive to be bad "government" leadership in America is a terrorist in the new interpretation of the word terrorist. If you were born in America, you are now a suspect every time you get on an airplane of being associated with Al Qaeda. Those fingernail clippers could be used to hijack a commercial airliner; that toothpaste and acne medication could be explosives in disguise. Why would anyone oppose what the people who are the United States government do, right? Jesus had NOTHING to do with the writing of the old or revised constitutions. Just because political corruption is over 4,000 years old in practice, there is NO cosmic "order" stating that political corruption has to continue until Jesus "comes back" (which is a billion trillion to the billionth power to one long gone shot), to "save us" from our own free will decisions. People who oppose radical changes being militarily forced on them (Iraq, Iran, Pakistan,

Afghanistan, etc.) by "outside forces" (a competitively divided United States with some allied help) whose leaders and chief capitalists want the oil, gas, and tax revenues from the developing economies; do have the right to put up resistance; any form of resistance they can come up with. What we call terrorism is actually self defense. Everyone who is born in this world has the right to exist, and "some people" do infringe on the abilities of others to enjoy life. Everyone has room for endless self-improvement; however, "some people" have decided they do not need any form of improvement, which is of course NOT true, we are all impure.

The largest part of the entire socio political economic problem is that certain people (the ones who are the government) collects trillions in tax revenues every year, year after year for decades, and waste most of what is collected with bad decisions and self serving one world government driven programs, horrible management problems, large scale in house stealing and embezzling, fraud (i.e. Medicare fraud, IRS frauds), poor training resulting in accidents and crashes of hundreds of billions of dollars of foreign terrorist defense equipment every year for decades, i.e. F-14 & 16 fighter jets, Blackhawk and other helicopters, B-52 bombers and other jets, space shuttles, etc., and 10,000 other everyday "areas" of excessive tax money waste; i.e. the $2,300.00 White House hammer that costs $20.00 at Wal-Mart, all the "giveaways" to foreigners who hate us, and other forms of corruption at every level. NO government group of employees from Indiana needs to go to a location out of Indiana to "discuss" economic problems that exist in Indiana. Such "trips" ARE of course at the taxpayer's expense. And they (Indiana or any "state" group who lives off tax money) call themselves "public servants;" (and the American people fall for it!). After 200 plus years of "serving" the public, every American should have a college education (a REAL EDUCATION, not a slave training brainwashing "education" in hypocrisy), and a worthwhile, good paying job. This business of stealing other people's stuff as a way of life has to end. Criminal behavior should have been eliminated at least 90% in the last 50 years, but that is not the case. Education is the key to the Human dilemma, and education is something people have to want. Education should be serious fun. Pressure to perform academically should be eliminated. Teaching to the grand satisfaction of everyone involved should be the highest objective, as compared to the 2010 tax based slave training education. We have to get off the same old repetitive track that always leads back to war and the erosion of public morality, ethics, integrity, and honesty. Many police officers SHOULD be in prison.

After the chemical process that created Earth (our air, water, dirt, and the processes that maintain this atmosphere; fire, ice, plants, etc.), there is almost no such thing as "free" after being born. We are all slaves to the environments; the natural environment, and the man made environments. Criminal behavior is a relative to natural psychological malfunctioning unless you are a weed personality type. America is a psychologically malfunctioning society, and "our" current two in one team of leaders cannot lead anyone anywhere other than to a place that is just like the current state of America. I am an American and I have paid for the right to tell anyone anywhere what "I think" about America. If you do not like listening to me, don't. Nonetheless, the fact remains; America is a mess. The insight I have been forced to accept assures me that my perspective is a missing link in the puzzle that could lead to the invention of a process that can be used to figuratively pave some old chuck holes in the thinking of the leaders in America that keep reappearing in the same old roads, and in every new road.

No business in America, as we all know, could survive if the business operated like the U.S. government; this is a fact (except for the military force's involvement). The only reason the government of any nation is under attack by anyone is because government "leaders" are corrupt. In reality, taxpayers are forced to spend billions every year for security programs to protect government employees from everyone else; including their own citizens. The day may be coming when masses of American citizens will have to DEMAND their rights and money with interest at gunpoint and by terrorist attack (if needed) until "the government" focuses on the needs of Americans BEFORE trying to save the rest of world from reproducing its own destruction. Carrying signs, chanting cliché's, and signing petitions will accomplish the equivalent of nothing, except maybe getting "a promise" to debate the issue on the house floor, a process that could take 15 years. In the mean time, thousands of millions suffer over $100.00 a week. Reproducing poverty and desperation has to stop. Arresting congress, the private family owners of "the federal reserve," and 5,000 or more IRS leaders, managers and their families; and confiscating their excess assets would be a good move to set a new example. Americans could then begin to collect from the bankers, CEO's and leaders of the big corporations who have robbed the people in what "THEY" call a "fair competitive playing field;" but that is by no means a fair playing field.

The U.S. government team of wise counsels (wise in their own eyes that is) WASTE more than enough money EVERY YEAR than what is needed to make EVERY American a millionaire. Don't get me wrong, as I said earlier, I am not into give away programs, I am for WORK and LEARN programs. This is not Africa, Mexico, China, or any other place. America is a land of potential, and so is every piece of the planet. Laziness, filth, crime, perversion, and at least 35% of "the things" Humans do have more negative reaction than positive and are social cancers; i.e. allowing uneducated, unemployed, children of criminals to reproduce Human life that is dependent on other poor people who already operate in a broken system. Teaching and rehabilitation are two primary areas for "new jobs," however, young Americans do not respect the older populations for being competent teachers (given the condition of the world, a fair and reasonable observation), and "young people" really do NOT have the knowledge, experience, and wisdom to teach those who are even younger. For example, there IS a difference between being "a government employee" and "a taxpayer." For one thing, government employees are paid from the wages of all other employees. Government employees do not contribute money to a pool that pays taxpayers. Tax is a one way street, the people who are the government say "you owe this much out of every transaction" and taxpayers pay. Government employees really do not pay taxes as their income is the tax money other people have already earned; and paid out of their paycheck to support government employees as they perpetuate the unjust tax system. Otherwise, taxpayers have little, few, or no rights, and government employees always have the upper hand in every situation. This is not democracy. Although I belong to no organization of any kind, I am not a friend of the people who are the United States government; it's a personality type thing. I have learned firsthand that except for congress, the president, governors, senators, and their staffs, U.S. government employees are not really serving anyone else. Government employees, managers, etc. cannot be trusted, and I am totally trustworthy. I am not a Mooslim, a Moslem, or a Muslim, and I am not a Baptist, Catholic, Mormon, or any other religious cult member. All churches have cult like features, and I do have an in-depth, in the past, "church history." Believe me, you do not want to "talk Bible" with me with the belief that YOU are going to tell ME what "it says." Better yet, I do not teach Bible Study for a price less than what is practical. Simply put, people are trained to fear truth, and I cannot remove the walls of fear that blind Humans from simple reality; I teach the truth, which is shocking. We are all here alone, individually; how we treat each other affects our molecular signature in the slurry of molecules that are the universe. There is no such thing as a prophet, or a person who can prove seeing Human life in another dimension of existence while in this one. I can see reason for a particle with rare crystals that reflect certain lights in the slurry of life like few other particles, but a Human born particle (Jesus) that can know all the answers to every Human question and more and then be killed by the taxing bodies and church leaders over a few words?

Don't let my name scare you, it is only a cosmic coincidence that my name sounds like how people are told to pronounce Al Qaeda (Al' KI 'duh). Al Kida is NOT pronounced like al kayda, al keeda, al kwada, al kweeda, al kwaydo, or any other "distraction focus" pronunciation (as in a rock, e rock, a rack, e rack, ih rock, ih rack, ear rock, and ear rack for Iraq, or I Rack). Yes, it was "the Greeks" who devised many of the first "rules" for using vowel and consonant sounds. Al Kida sounds just like it looks, "Al" like in "Big AL, the gang leader;" short for Allen; and Kida has a LONG I sound like in "I" just typed the words you are reading. Not Kid (like "Billy the Kid" a), "I" like in Idaho. Al Kida. I am not a terrorist, but I am accused and suspected of being one (on a list) made by the U.S. government (who is also very interested in a good friend of mine, a neighbor who has an extensive history with the IRS, FBI, and other government offices). In reality, Americans need me on America's side in any battle where Americans are attacked, including attacks in America by Americans preying on Americans (America's biggest crime problem). Socialism, capitalism, democracy, religion, gender, and skin color can't change Human attitudes relative to individual Human behavior. Rather, people have attitudes about such topics. Human trust is almost dead in America, and respect is all but vanished. I want a new democracy, limits on extremist, greedy, capitalism (like an Exxon executive making a $400 million dollar bonus during an alleged period of short supply), full time employment for everyone in worthwhile jobs, "health care" (largely diet and exercise programs) for everyone, quality food, clean good clothing and shelter for everyone, clean drinking water, co-operation to replace competition, earn and learn college degrees and work study programs for everyone, an end to war, a cleaner environment, and respect for all things.

We are all learning, but what are we learning? I am an engineer, however, as you can tell, I do not talk like an engineer; which is something that hurt my career with a large firm; it's a personality type thing, believe me. Besides, now that I know, I am much better off as an independent. I am not a weapons or explosives engineer like my name might suggest. I am also not a pilot with religion based suicidal tendencies. And, I most certainly would never commit suicide and murder in the name of some primitive man made god or any current government philosophy. I am angry at America, and with good cause. For example, I am practically surrounded by people, who; without knowing what they are doing, are actually acting out a daily "worship" service to the ancient Human mythological god (a real man) called Chaos, who "sired the egg" that became Phanes, a hermaphrodite with creative abilities. In this sense, "worship" means "faithfully adhere to practices and pre-programmed beliefs in a limited perspective of life alternatives by perpetuating the pre-programming without question or personal research." Perpetuating capitalism in its current state is the same as perpetuating and multiplying chaos (confusion that leads to unhappy lives). Few people know how Chaos, (ancient Greek strategist); like Zeus (ancient womanizer and politician) used "confusion" (ancient media, word of mouth, scripts) as a secret weapon in negotiations; i.e. "one group" of people convince a lesser developed nation that becoming slaves to them will improve the standard of living for all people of the other nation when exploitation of the people and the land by the "one group" is the real objective. In ancient times, "one group" of people would promise all sorts of improvements, gain confidence, then kill the lesser developed group, depending on various factors, i.e. age differentials, gender, appearance, learning skills, religious worship ceremony acts, etc. Here is a hard part of the story if you don't already know; in ancient times "the church was the state." Today, when you take the paranoid, self deception explanation away from "the reasoning" law makers use to justify their bad decisions, the church becomes the state again; i.e. alleged morality, ethics, and integrity are deceptively woven into rhetoric that describes a philosophy of "forgiveness" AFTER adherence "to the law in a democratic constitutional forum" (that really does NOT exist). Killing over money, land, minerals, sex act preference, skin color, and other reproduced and perpetuated religious belief systems allegedly found in primitive writings is not doing anything more than perpetuating social decay. Every surviving nation in Human history goes through changes in time, from being a few thousand "patriots and zealots" to becoming a "great" (in Humans terms) nation, and finally; every past "great nation" ends up being destroyed. America is headed down the destruction highway at a high speed in a Corvette being driven by a drunk congressman out on a date with a girl friend, a pretty girl, not his wife; trying to impress his date with his new driving skills in a freezing rain on wet streets by a dangerous bridge in a bend on the road. (Defining "great" in Human terms is a personality type situation specific issue as in a describing a "great" symphony as compared to a "great" gender and skin color hate based "rap" that thump duh dumps like 99% of most other rap. Great?"). That we exist, THAT is great.

The fact that we exist is so far beyond everything Humans think is great (Human produced machines and technology) that we could (should) be more focused on inventing harmonious relations with ALL PEOPLE instead of focusing on Human pride and self proclaimed Human greatness. Being in a position to collect large sums of money, own numerous homes, cars, and other possessions does not constitute any right to a cosmic advantage over beings that have nothing other than the clothes on their backs. Truth is, Humans do not know and cannot know all of the laws of the universe. No primitive book can pave the way to eternal life for Humans; but having a clear, positive, help anyone "attitude" does seem to have some long term positive effects in this temporary stage of life.

Chaos is a state of mind. To prove this to yourself, stop everything for a few moments and just listen to all the noise in your head that comes from outside sources; i.e. a commercial jingle, sports statistics, grocery list, my hair, my car, this engine, that bra, my bank account, my debt, the things kids do today that we never did when we were children, we need more toilet paper and kitty litter, the house payment is due in three days, the electric bill went up, the septic tank needs to be pumped again, property tax is due next month, the courts released a serial rapist from prison yesterday due to a flaw in the evidence presentation process at trial, and on and on it goes, chaos. Of all the distractions, the vanity and sex based "language of denial" (that the media and politicians use to define capitalism, the stock market, socialism, important news, idol worship, religion, the flow of money, sex, sports, drugs, crime, fashion, birthdays, big lips and gigantic mouths with long tongues chomping dead animal meat sandwiches, tax lawyers who were once IRS agents making deals, traditional celebrations remade into tax collection celebrations, etc.); IS the greatest seducer and brainwashing tool (the language of denial) known to manipulative deceivers. Politicians are top notch manipulative deceivers; it's a personality type thing.

(Small jump of focus to make a common point). We are all seduced by the potential of beautiful women, so why not make everything a display that suggests a connection between "our product" and the potential of a beautiful woman? Even if the view of a pretty female face is seen from inside a toilet bowl looking out in a discussion over "which cleaning product to use;" a capitalist will smell the "value" from a sales based foundation (based on government research for sales tax revenues) and everyone allegedly "wins." (The advertising agency gets paid, the company selling the product gets paid and the CEO gets a huge bonus, the consumer has a cleaner toilet, millions of people saw the pretty female face from inside the toilet, income tax was collected on every individual involved, sales tax is collected on every bottle sold, everyone is happy, capitalism and democracy are great for selling toilets and all the tools and chemicals associated with having three in the house; the "actress" gets paid and has added paid experience to her resume). The questions relative to capitalism in this subject area are, do people need to be reminded that toilets have to be cleaned? Why was a White female face seen from inside the toilet? How much did the commercial increase the cost of the product? Why would anyone create a toilet cleaning product that didn't work? Do we really need to see toilets on the television for any reason? "There are no toilets in heaven" (quote by JP Freije).

People swishing mouth wash in their big mouths and craving animal fluid dripping burgers are other over used gross forms of capitalist powers; i.e. studies show that sales of certain products increase when the ads show people sticking spoons of whatever (cereal, pudding, sloppy burgers with cheese, etc.) into their mouths. How very shallow is that? Abusive capitalism can be summed up by cartoon character sex symbols, toilet cleaning commercials, and (dead ground up) all beef cow (muscle tissue) burger chewing commercials. Tax is a coming in and going out proposition. Tax revenue drives this new one world American government (McDonalds, Coke, Pepsi in China and India) plan, which is a corrupt competitive militarized capitalist police state, not a democracy or a republic. Webster defines a republic as: a state or nation in which the supreme power rests in all the citizens entitled to vote and is exercised by representatives elected by them. Fact is, even though the elected representatives are elected, the vote is not a majority vote representation as claimed, simply because the majority of the people do not have faith in either of the two competing political parties and do not vote. The people with the most "Human power" over money (congress, "the federal reserve," the IRS, tax courts, judges in general, lawyers, doctors, insurance companies, car companies, etc.) "take bribes" via lobbyists (payments in some form), the word bribe used as a figure of speech only; to write favorable to them (costly to consumers) clauses into laws that enable the companies paying the lobbyists to make more profit, which means "the government" (people whose products include taxes, bombs, mass murder, bad decisions of all kinds in every area of life) can collect more tax to build a better police state. When the IRS pursues individuals for 12 plus years over an alleged $55,000.00 (four trials, 9 judges, 16 IRS lawyers) that was proven to never have been due, while other individuals steal billions in Medicare fraud in just three years; is clear proof of a government out of control. Go to the Treasury Inspector General for Tax Administration (TIGTA) web site (www.tigta.gov); do a thorough search into the site and KNOW 95% of their bragging is based on LIES relative to their alleged ethics, integrity, fairness, honesty, and professionalism. Try and do a historical search on crimes committed by IRS employees, it is shocking what they do publish and admit; a couple hundred out of thousands of complaints every year. Take it from someone who knows firsthand, in your (my) face with guns, the IRS is a CRIMINAL OPERATION, and is a Trust that exists in Puerto Rico. All traditional celebrations are simply police and IRS monitored tax collecting government stimulus programs; i.e. Christmas, Easter, Halloween, birthdays, etc.; these are fuels that perpetuate taxation, excessive wasteful spending, chaos, and distractions that keep people from learning higher knowledge. (Just about everything is police monitored these days, including learning and internet porn. Yes, the FBI gets paid with tax dollars to watch pornography, looking for criminal suspects and missing young sex slave girls). Remember, holidays are not holy days to the universe, only to Humans.

What is capitalism? What is democracy? According to Webster's New World dictionary, capitalism is an economic system in which the means of production and distribution are privately owned and operated for a profit, originally under fully competitive conditions. Privately owned now means by large corporations more so than by small companies, families, or individuals. Also, capitalism is "the principles, and or powers of capitalists." In reality, there is no such thing as "fully competitive" any more, everything is a chaotic scramble for the most money as fast as possible from every transaction. Large corporations can afford to buy new inventions and put the small man or woman inventor out of business quickly, with help from lawyers. A person really has to have some money in order to make more money; which they have to fight to keep. Face it, capitalism has become what it is, well planned double talking competitive deception with blood and guts over money; because Humans lack real knowledge of their purpose in the universe. My recent experiences with Hewlett Packard (HP) and Best Buy was a capitalist one world economy experience at its finest. In short, the defective HP computer and printer system we purchased at Best Buy (being sold as "the latest and greatest thing on the market") was defective in 33 days after purchase. The system is made in Thailand and Taiwan, sold in the U.S., programmed in the U.S., and repaired in Canada (printers) or in Arkansas (tower). The Geek Squad at Best Buy had three opportunities to fix the problems but they could not do so in house and would need five or six weeks to fix a newly sold (less than 45 days old) system. After two hours on the phone, Hewlett Packard said "you need a new printer, give us your charge card number and we will send you another new one." When the "tower" was taken the third time to Best Buy, a Geek Squad guy sprayed a chemical on a fan and said the problem was fixed; it was not fixed. I was told to "buy another system" while the other new system was being repaired. If the first new computer was fixed within the 30 day return period, I could return the second new computer. Hewlett Packard and Best Buy both agreed that 5-6 weeks of work DOWN TIME as the result of a defective computer was "nothing to get excited about." In order to duplicate the original computer system for my personal use, I had to add a variety of programs. If the new first computer was not repaired in 30 days, and if I did not return the second system until 32 days later, I now owned two new computers. What a marketing strategy by Hewlett Packard and Best Buy. I will NEVER own another HP anything, or buy anything from Best Buy again. I even had an extended warranty.

After several efforts to arrange a workable resolution with Best Buy to no avail, I contacted an HP warranty licensed "Geek" company, who came to the house, solved nothing, and wanted $200.00. HP had sent the wrong repair part, the Geek could not do the job, which took him over two hours to realize. When HP sent the right part, I changed it in 15 minutes. This is just one small example of "the powers" of capitalists; make computer systems dependent on international economic relations, and keep the relations in a state of constant political chaos until "OUR Lord" comes back and gives US everything good we think we deserve.

"Perpetuating chaos" is brainwashing in action as in "we will tell you how this is to be viewed." Cramming sex down the throats of children (or in their minds with adult talk, behavior, books, magazines, television, the internet, cartoons, young adult teacher leadership, etc.) will eventually result in historical repetition of an embarrassing kind. America will not be the first nation to "get caught" by an underestimated, under ranked enemy with their "pants off" (looking at a Penthouse magazine instead of a radar screen, having sex when you should be standing guard). This is a literal interpretation of history. It is an indisputable fact that many "primitive" peoples "worshipped" their "god" with ceremonial and ritualized orgiastic drunkenness (getting drunk and having an orgy as a religious ritual). In fact, the leaders of the first greatest peoples, the original primitives who mastered and perfected gold refinement over 3,000 years ago, stone cutting, wood working, ship and furniture building, art, etc. were caught with their pants down "during worship service." The history of these truly great people is denied and covered up, looked over, and called by other names. Without the protection of the Phrygians, there would be no Israel. Humans change stories as the stories get repeated, and a great deal of "the whole story" gets lost rather quickly (which depends on who is telling the story). What happened in ancient civilizations is almost 100% open for in general interpretation. Expert analysis is often conjecture and speculation with a shot in the dark accuracy. We are in the dark about our oldest ancestors. Most Humans, and most sub-Humans, can detect progression and change; it is an inborn ability for all independently moving organisms (birds fly south for the winter, salmon swim upstream, whales migrate to give birth and become pregnant, etc.). Beware of people who are eager to tell you what to believe and why; i.e. extraverts, republicans, democrats, Christians, Muslims, police, military, congress, IRS, etc. Where the Human spirit (life memory cells; electro magnetically charged conglomeration of highly specialized molecules that exist in a Human body (a by-product of what we call nuclear energy) "goes" after this life is yet to be known. However, in the subtleness of the stillness, on a molecular level, there are some obvious indicators of an electromagnetic web of electrically charged "veins and strings" that form a web that touches and exists in everything everywhere, no matter how far away; for example, hundreds of trillions of light years in Human measuring scales.

Primitives learned to count days and nights, and seasonal change began to show a pattern within so many days of the same count on an annual basis; i.e. how the primitives named the "equinox" periods. America is "not there yet," relative to the act of sex and child sacrifice being performed live on an alter in American churches four times a year every year, but the world can see our satellite programs, and it looks like we are having an orgy when we should be policing the police, congress, the courts, the lawyers' associations across the country, the IRS, and other war mongering, manipulative self deceivers and paranoid incompetents. Stand back, and look, in public; America has sex, drug, law, sports, religion, communication, and education problems (and many leadership problems, tax problems, chaos based everyday dollar problems, etc.). And, we are all "free" allegedly to change things.

According to Webster, democracy is "government by the people, or through elected representatives, a majority rule, the acceptance and practice of the principle of equality of rights, opportunity, and treatment." However, just like in 1775, the "elected representatives" today 2010 do not represent "the majority of the people," but instead represent the people with the most money, a minority, at the expense of the majority. On average less than half of the people vote, that less than half is divided at least three ways, so the majority of the people are never really represented. Any claim to the contrary is self serving. Why don't people vote? Because nothing ever changes that helps life be more fun for more people regardless of who is in the white house. There is a lot of fun, laughter, and happiness in the world that is not being used or expressed. Democrats and Republicans throwing the exact same stones at each other has never solved anything, but it has made some politicians very wealthy, and primarily it is the working class who gets hit with the stones being thrown by the leaders of both parties. The same issues (pollution, taxes, the economy, abortion, crime, drugs, global warming, war, sex act preference, skin color, and all the forms of hate and abuse against women, etc.) are most generally on the surface these days, and the only difference in the argument that is allegedly focused on a resolution to the problem is who calls who liberal or conservative, or moderate, or independent, or left or right. Why are the "most conservative" also the most willing to kill in war, the least willing to kill in an abortion (allegedly abortion is liberal) while liberals are allegedly anti-war, pro-abortion? Chaos gets people elected. People most generally really do not know why they believe what they believe. Abortion sounds horrible to me, and I have never been involved as a party to an abortion. When the heartbeat starts (only minutes after the sperm cracks the egg), the universe is open to forming a new life inside a like kind, a link in the invisible universal web of electrical impulse that holds this dimension of existence together. Why? Perhaps so our "impulse collector" will grow and become a form through which higher life forms can get a glimpse of the greatness of our Creator through the eyes of lowly but somewhat sophisticated organisms like us Humans. Humans are simply highly specialized big bacteria; Human bacteria. Our slimy molecular structures have to go through a refinement process to prepare us for our real future. We cannot walk into heaven smelling like a Human. As long as we produce waste products, we Humans are not ready for passage into a cleaner environment. How much money we had on Earth is irrelevant in molecular coding, Heaven is a place with unknown to us molecular code marking only a higher than Human power can read. Waste cannot exist in a perfect place.

Okay, I cannot deny that abortion is a free will choice matter. If the universe has a way to deal such activity, the universe will deal with it. I am convinced the universe is totally capable of dealing with everything that happens in this universe on every level, including the microscopic level; and that everything is dealt with accordingly, according to the laws of the universe, where we live, not the laws of congress that do not apply to congress. Some lines do have to be drawn in allowing certain behaviors, such as the perverted behavior of adults having sex with children; and having children act out adult sex fantasies and problems on television sitcom's; and in cartoons. People can't see the forest for the trees, or the deception and insanity of the brainwashing for the television commercials.

Up until the early mid 1500's, before the great Copernicus, the belief of the state run church, and church run state, was that the Sun moved around the Earth and that Human "kings" and governments through bloodline were at the control center of the universe. Yea, and the moon is made of garlic flavored sour cottage cheese. Copernicus was accused of blasphemy for proposing that the Earth moved around the Sun, and a bounty (price) was put on his head. Copernicus tried to explain the "math error" in the previous calculations, more charges were levied, and Copernicus fled underground. On a side note, another thing "the government" has covered up (edited out of school books) is that the famous Galileo died in prison as a result of his defense of Copernicus. Galileo was given the studies of Copernicus, and later, after much study, agreed with Copernicus, which was devastating to the kings of the time who thought they knew without doubt that "they" were at the center of the universe; much like how kings, queens, presidents, congressmen and women, lawyers, senators, bankers, insurance companies, media companies, and giant corporation "leaders" in general "think" today. The attitude that "I have to be a leader!" is a personality type issue; and this "type" of person is virtually everywhere seeking to use their self overrated job position authority to bully and intimidate their way "to the top." No one Human being needs a billion dollars.

Galileo was told by the church and state leaders "if you denounce Copernicus, we will set you free." Believing (and knowing) Copernicus was correct, Galileo could not denounce him, and Galileo died in prison; Copernicus died while in hiding. The government "attitude of today" existed long before America. Can't you hear the "state" telling Galileo "You WILL lie to the public to save the face of your pope and the other church leaders, and the state leaders, and then we will let you out of prison. We can cover up the mess until long after all of us have passed on. The knowledge will come forward in time in part, it will give people something to talk about and try and figure out for decades. Let's just leave it alone until after we are gone and let nature take its course, it's a tradition." How would a council of leaders "cover up" an issue like what innocent Copernicus discovered; Earth moves around the Sun? Sweep the matter "under the rug?" Create MORE Chaos? Legislate a new law and tax? Put on a show and fake a miracle to demonstrate "the power" of the church and state? (Give a child the power of the King, claim the child changed the heavens, and now the Earth is moving around the sun. This way, the child king will, with intense protection, live a long time, allowing the adults in charge to further their tax revenue embezzling schemes that increase the size of their (in secret) retirement packages). Stealing, lying, killing, and being lazy are possible behaviors, but engaging in such behaviors is a free will issue. We do not have to act out every potential Human behavior to know that some behaviors are not positive (just because others got away with the same thing for years). An untrained dog will find a lifetime of mischief.

Chaos and Zeus were perceived to have super Human or "god like" abilities, which we all should know is exaggerated, like the power of congress, the president, all the church leaders, all the corporations, all the CEO's, and the majority of the people. We all know people with the personality type of "I'm the King!" and "I'm the Queen!" Other Greek "gods" were named Cybele, and Dionysus (the two greatest primitive Phrygian gods), Ares, Diana, Atlas, Aphrodite, Cupid, Pluto, Phoebus, Vulcan, Hestia,

Janus, Hermes, and many others. Chaotic "god" worship was a form of invisible self destruction mental disease created by the ancients; they just could not know what we know today. The "Big Bang" theory DOES coincide with Creation theory IF you know how to understand. The quest to understand our existence is in a state of God overload, which does opiate the masses. No one by the names of Jesus (Baptist, Catholic, etc., etc.), Allah (Shiite, Sunni, etc., etc.), Buddha, Krishna, Nhialic, Kwoth, Nyame, or other man made gods is going to come back and save all of us who believe in him or her from the laws of universal chemical reaction. This entire perceivable existence is the result of an electromagnetic chemical reaction. Something with far more intelligence than Humans "invented" the chemicals and engineering that became and maintains this daily existence. The "nuclear energy" that is our source of life transforms us, and at this level, we have a lot of troubles through which we need to transform. If a few of us had any real idea of what is required to transform microscopic materials into a Human Being, then the rest of us would have better lives; I mean much better lives, emphasis on "much better." We are independent electrical components that add connectivity into the universe for future potential use in this environment. We are all connected to each other electrically, and a part of all of us flows through the same types of life's layered obstacles. Money helps people get through the troubles of life at this level with more ease than without money. The best health care plan is a good diet and regular exercise. What is a good diet is the issue for some. I am a strict no meat, no egg, no milk, no by-products of dairy products, very light alcohol drinker, no soda drinking, several supplement taking health nut diet eater. I drink coffee, tea, reverse osmosis filtered water, a few different sports drinks, and cranberry juice.

The man god Chaos showed an army of "powerful" people how to seize control of prized real estate by using diplomatic confusion to accomplish their objectives (in primitive times, objectives were to have the finest gold, furniture, cloth, marble, wine, the most women, children, allies, slaves, soldiers, and armed tax collectors). Throughout time, information overload leads to chaotic behavior, which opens doors where deception can enter virtually undetected for long periods, and in time, persuasions of all kinds become "programmable," like turning an innocent, abused 15 year old girl into a gang bang porn "star." "It's all right honey," the pro's say, "it's the oldest profession known to mankind, you will always have work to do, men and women will love you." Now the programming mixes the concepts of sex and war and more sex with murder. We become more competitive, deeper in blind denial, more violent, and more "intelligent" with our murderous sex and money lies, until the infighting escalates and we start consuming each other. Jesus was not murdered so WE could "be forgiven," he was murdered because kings were afraid of what he might say to the public that would cause a revolt (disrupt the tax income flow). All the while, "our allies" and our enemies are looking at America as THE NUMBER ONE target for Earth cleansing eradication; while also trying to deny some of their own problems, and planning to utilize, in part, American methods to resolve their conflicts. Americans are not the smartest or dumbest people on Earth, however, as a group, Americans are obviously the most willing to kill of the alleged civilized nuclear bomb armed nations. There are still primitive tribes on planet Earth, who on a very small scale, are more willing to kill than most Americans, but they are small and an exception. In some cultures, still today, Humans are eaten and their blood drank. Eating bodies and drinking blood happened long before Christ. In other words, GODS do not draw property lines along any borders of Human religious, political, skin color, or gender philosophies. "Either do it our way or we will blow you up and invade your country and blame you for everything until you give up" is NOT "diplomacy."

A well planned chaotic information overload with Machiavellian style cover up is generally successful, given the power of media. Media focus in part is used to distract direct examination of political, religious, and economic cause and effect. What the majority of the people on planet Earth do not know is that the few (percentage wise) are willing to blow up the rest of the world to save themselves. The truth hurts "some people", and those people will block the rightful progress of others who tell the truth regardless of who "gets hurt." "If the truth makes you feel stupid, the truth is not the problem." (quote by JP Freije).

Americans are masters at telling, believing, and perpetuating traditional lies. Yes, the police can and do deny using excessive force, even if the video tape proves otherwise. Police officers can, do, and will LIE under oath to cover their asses when they make an error that cost an innocent person a large sum of money, trouble, and heart ache. The police can always find a "good" defense lawyer. There IS a balance point for all things, or else none of us would be here. Money and math go together like water and moisture, but the water puddles up a lot faster in a few places, and never touches other parts of the same area. In essence, I write because the world needs a truth revolution. The images from the words I use do not always present a pretty picture, but you should not be insulted by anything said in this book. The revolution some Americans are expecting or denying will take place will not be discussed or commercially advertised until long after that revolution is well under way. American communication networks are very vulnerable. Al Kida also knows that America is under attack, the plan barely unfolded, and this Al Kida is certainly NOT a player in any plan to undermine anything except deception. America IS the number one target of an international based covert attack. Overt attacks could erupt. This is not a threat, but a FACT. I am NOT involved other than being able to see what is going on; you don't have to listen.

America has problems with Africa, inside and out of America, like with Mexico, with Iraq, Iran, Pakistan, the Soviet Union, Afghanistan, Al Qaeda (not Al Kida in the same sense), Venezuela, Cuba, and on and on it goes. Al Kida IS a threat to tell as much of the truth (freedom of speech) as what he KNOWS from up close firsthand personal eye and ear witness experience with many people, particularly U.S. government employees. Al Kida and no one he knows has any reason to deceive anyone. No dead prophet can come back and save us from our own failures to educate and care for each other better than we have. Taking advantage of the lesser fortunate is NOT something the universe does as a natural function. Building a Human brain and body from microns is NOT easy, especially the way some bodies look, and given the tolerance levels of the design.

I, Al Kida, am not involved in any plot to harm anyone anywhere. Also, I am not religious. I do not believe in a hell, I believe that the creator(s) of our universe are good, and would not "burn a soul FOREVER" because a soul didn't "believe in HIS" only "Son or Prophet." Permanently turn off the lights in your molecular essence and use your remains as fill material in space cracks, yes; but burn you FOREVER, no. There is no sense in that, no good, no love, no compassion, no sense at all. And the "believe in" part; Jesus just re-packaged the spiritual philosophies of the Stoics who preceded him. Jesus was a Stoic of a unique kind, a very unique personality, but he is not "coming back" to save anyone from all the bad choices in using their free will. I do not want to be involved in any fight, civil war or world war relative to what someone else thinks, wants, or think they need at the cost of other Human life, as in "you die so I can get what I want in the name of my god."

Like my parents and two of my grandparents, I was born in America. I have always lived and worked in America, am educated in America, have a high standard, but not elaborate anything. My business ethics and integrity are beyond reproach, and I refuse to let unscrupulous people (in America) take advantage of me if I can prevent such activity, but the courts and churches favor self proclaimed "repentant" criminals in America, as compared to truly smart hard working honest people. Look at congress *for* example (of criminal leadership; NOT as **an** example like in "setting an example for innocent children to model in THEIR behavior"), of criminals who go to church. I have no faith in any church or political party, label, cliché, or stereotype. I have faith in my concept of the creator(s) of the universe. If anyone is going to die for MY (your) sins it should be me dying for mine, and you dying for yours. I could not let anyone die for something I have done that most people would think deserves the death penalty as the only form of punishment. There is no person on Earth, in my opinion, who has the GOD, God, or god given right to decide that anyone should be killed, except in self defense, and then ONLY if some other measure cannot be used first; i.e. disable with other means, from chemical, electric shock, to physical means if needed, put in prison, but never excessive gang bang put him in handcuffs then kick and beat the crap out of him force. There are a lot of Human monsters out there, and Human monsters need to be controlled to an extreme. Some monsters wear suits and ties, other wear military or police uniforms, a doctor's gown and gloves and mask, a judge's robe, a g-string and make up, or the typical everyday dress of any American or worldwide Human from preacher to teacher, babysitter, lawyer, judge, or congressman. Monsters are everywhere, and many of them do think, believe, and act like Charles Manson; as in "I don't like those people, they participated in blocking my way of getting into the big money flow. I want you to go kill them, it's your patriotic duty." At the same time, anyone who thinks they can speak for GOD; don't tell me about it. Just because "the law" will allow the police, soldiers, and criminals, for example; to kill someone and claim a variety of defenses, it does not mean the eyes of the universe did not see what happened. No Human can hide anything from the eyes of the universe, never ever. I am confident the universe has a way to rectify forced on unjustified suffering associated with every negative function (such as murdered life; abortion, war, drunk driving, or street fight related death) where innocent people experience pain and loses due to rich kids fighting over more money or sex, or poor people killing over meth and alcohol. Remember, every Human is connected to an invisible to Humans electrical mesh of molecular structures with an electro-magnetic chemical memory connected to an infinite power source that has a record of everything. We are like blips on a screen, a dot in infinity with nuclear capability, living breathing, able to love or hate, lie or tell the truth; and look at what we do, fight over things, and reproduce and perpetuate our own stupidity.

I was taught to defend myself, and to not go looking for fights; and to redirect my sexual energy into intellectual pursuits. Yes, I was a strange child to some. As a young adult, I learned firsthand what it meant to never do anything that would warrant a death penalty or any prison sentence (and especially nothing that would warrant forcing myself to psychologically construct my philosophical life foundation around carrying and displaying the Christian fear of alleged eternal life in a fiery traditional hell). I have enough trouble on a daily basis with my name that I feel like I'm already in warm up camp for a type of hell; and I am a good person by any positive set of standards. Christians pretend to be my friends all the while waiting, looking, and trying to create a situation from which they can attack me with words and make me defend myself. Muslims are happy as long as I don't pressure them about religion. But, that praying in a group thing three times a day, I get the drift, but give me a break; talk about zealots. I "talk to GOD" all day every day. I blame GOD for allowing all the little things in my life that bug me (like other people's lousy driving, bad attitudes in general, greed, lies, willingness to cheat to get money, etc.). Then there are 10,000 arguments about "everyone having the right to live!" The right to live and using free will recklessly are two different arguments. I did my share of stupid stuff in my misguided youth, but I was a misguided young man with tremendous potential I was not allowed to utilize. This Al Kida is pro life; Human and animal life. Relax, I do not know Al Qaeda or any of its members. I have paid my dues in life, and then some (so it seems), and I am not a criminal. I believe there is a workable corrective position to every Human malfunction, issue, and condition. NOTE: You and I are responsible for putting "a tone" to these words; your reading tone and my writing tone may not match; so don't be too judgmental relative to what you think I may be saying. Certain "key" words DO evoke a "conditioned" response (a pre-conditioned position of perception influenced by parents, extended families, co-workers, peer pressure, television, fear, church, etc. rather than by personal endeavor) as in the assumed belief that "MOST people believe what I believe." There is such a thing as comfort and safety in numbers, but if everyone believes the same old lie as a foundation for everything else, the effort is largely a waste (misdirected use) of good energy. However, potential for corrective action exists, due to the "safety in numbers" factor; which is also now challenged due to a loss of national cohesiveness (every state has individual problems) that re-surfaced while the ongoing failures of our government employee leadership became more exposed. We have to face our problems head on. Fighting needs to be replaced with co-operation; which is easier said than done, due to the attitudes of "some people," largely republicans, democrats, and media representatives. There are few things "most people believe" in unison, other than issues such as heat is hot, water is wet, granite is hard, the sun is very bright, Human blood is red, and other such things. Any way we look at it, except from the eyes of the law makers and law enforcers (people whose salaries and benefits are the taxes, fines, and fees levied on the people who are not paid from taxes, fines, and fees), the majority of the American people who do not work for the government support all of the people who are the government, AND most of the sick, unemployed, destitute, in trouble Humans around the world. Making half of the masses pay for the failures and excesses of the other half is NOT an example of a healthy, functioning democracy; or a display of mature behavior that is driven by an intelligent force that exists in our realm of perception. What we don't know can kill us, and "some people" want to limit knowledge. We cannot always see who is watching us, but we are being watched from great distances, and close up. I have alien tendencies.

I have travelled to several foreign lands and seas, have a four year college degree with Honors, and a successful self-employment one man operation engineering business. So cutting to the last race of the chase, we have a Human problem on our hands. If you can read this, you are Human; and, you have the potential to do all things good, or all things that are considered evil; or a mix of the two (usually fake "good" to hide the real evil). Making an excessive competitive greed commission on every transaction is like burning a candle at both ends, the business of the candle will burn up faster as compared to just burning one end (you may have to find another candle). All life exists in its own molecular core frequency range. To the best of my Human knowledge, only Humans and more sophisticated beings that exist in the invisible to Humans dimensions of the infinite electromagnetic web can read these words and know what they mean. Humans have never seen or identified the unique set of nuclear molecules that control Human brain function. Our Human Bodies are carrying cases for a small portion of what we call a by-product of nuclear energy; or nuclear waste by-products, us; Humans, by products of waste from what we call nuclear waste. Technically, our sun is nuclear waste, in Human terms.

When the sperm breaks through the protective coating and shell and wiggle swims into the egg, infinite space and time are temporarily open for expansion. Nuclear energy floods the available space, opening the genetic locks and releasing the pre-programming in the atoms of the new life particle donators. When a heart beat starts, in minutes, there is new life in progress and the cell openings to the power of the universe are closed, as enough "nuclear waste" dripped into GOD's little secret to form a new Human body that could live at least to age 150 (years), if maintained. Barring abortion or other pre-mature death, nine months later, a new Human carrying case for pre-programmed nuclear memory energy erupts through existing flesh. Skin color, gender, grandparents' religious beliefs, sex preference, type of government in the country of the new life, economic status of the "parents," etc. are irrelevant to the universe. What matters is that there is another Human on the Earth, another link between the future and the present, the past stored away in memory cells, but still in the brain and blood. A direct electro-molecular connection to the universal electromagnetic web is the same as a connection to the power that is still in the process of creating infinity; and every Human has a built in connection to this power, on the molecular level. Look at what some Humans do with this potential. In my opinion, figuratively speaking, GOD recycles our molecular materials (memory storage atoms, experience collector cells) into different life formats until the essence of each individual life is refined into a diamond or dust. I am trying for the diamond, and trying to get out of the dust bowl. While some people struggle for pleasure in this world, I seek pleasure in worlds beyond this world, that exist in dimensions connected to this world. Some say I am a dreamer, and that I think too much. I am simply sick and fed up with seeing people suffer because of money and their own stupidity. I am even more fed up with seeing abusive people take economic advantage of others. The only way to teach abusive people how to not be abusive is to turn the abuse back on the abuser; if that doesn't cure them, prison is next.

Images on your television are by products of highly specialized beams of highly specialized light particles. What is highly specialized to us today is old old old news to the universe. You are a by-product of something that was a lot like you, who cares how long ago it was, now and forever is what we are after, right? The future is what counts, but a realistically accurate past is good to know. A question to consider, will your molecular structure become fill material for cracks in the walls of space of time, or will your molecular structure become a new being that lives forever in a dimension of life that is superior to life on Earth in many ways; i.e. no reason or need for a toilet, but still have a Human like body? Ask also, if there is an order in the ranking of life forms towards a "perfect" body (carrying case for nuclear memory cells), how many layers deep are the ranks of Humans compared to the next level of more refined "higher" beings? Being able to control individual behavior on every level of life seems to be a key element in all life progress, and the universe makes all the rules. Humans like to think we know the rules, and I have a lot to say about this, but now is not the time. All life seems to exist in a multi-dimensional spiraling spiritual soup slurry. Each lap around the sun is in a new dimension, one lap being one year, everyone travelling at the same speed; temporary passengers on a planet we call Earth. Each molecule in the slurry (soup in a blender as large or larger than the Milky Way) has the potential to self direct independent movement toward self-improvement, which has no limits. Certain elements in the soup rise to the top of the foam on the soup. You can live in the slurry forever if you like, but the greatest pleasure in life is to be in the foam on the soup, and anyone can achieve such a place. All life is spiritual. Dolphins and catfish both live in water, one water animal on the cleaner surface of the ocean, the other in the dark muddy water at the bottom of the river, lake, or pond. Perhaps we all have to spend time on every level.

One's inability (or refusal) to recognize (or admit) the spiritual nature of life is not a reason or an excuse for anyone to violently attempt to impose their attitude, belief system, etc. on anyone else, in my opinion. Realizing the spiritual nature of life is NOT the purpose of congress. The real purposes of congress are to legislate laws that collect taxes, fines, fees, use force and courts to allegedly justify the acts of pursuing taxes, fines, fees, and interest; while also generating revenue for government employee retirement programs, Medicare (which gave away over $98 Billion in 2009 to fraud), war, spying on Americans, etc.; AND expanding the "American government employee attitude" of control by force around the world with military and economic weapons in the name of democracy and a loving "God." A common explanation given by too many government employees about the lack of ethics, integrity, and professionalism in government work is; "it's my JOB!" and "Someone HAS TO do it!" It IS a fruitless BUSINESS; collecting taxes, fines, and fees; a one way street, dead end. The giant blood sucking tick tax, fine, and fee system is run by people who obviously do not know how to manage money, or solve problems with money, all they can do is collect the money with force, and too often with lies, and fraud; which leads to horrendous waste.

Realize this; "understanding" takes place in an invisible place. Waves of strings of electromagnetic energy far too small to measure are our source of life. Human bodies have an energy field, or a molecular configuration that is a receiver for a special kind of energy signal we cannot detect, like with the many signals we create ourselves. Molecular signatures are our source of vision, and the source of our other senses; and our intuition. Given that "sound is a vibration that carries information," perhaps you can hear the meaning in the sounds of the vibration in your own head when you read these words; hate, love, kill, love. Relative to your government, incompetence is up to code on just about every level of operation. Human potential is in handcuffs, too many people cannot be trusted. Primitive religion should not be needed for people to see the deception in Human political behavior. Corruption is common in government simply because government work is largely force and paperwork protected by "sovereign immunity" with no other explanation. Certain types of people genuinely DO enjoy using force to get "what they want," which is usually something someone else has invented or earned; including respect, a self funded retirement, a good reputation, etc.

Sending young, uneducated men and women to war in foreign lands under false and mislabeled pretense at taxpayer's expense does thin the population as desired by the planners; and war stimulates the economy, and opens up new avenues for capitalism and tax revenue collecting, but such behavior is founded in deep deception, corruption, and murder. Americans do not have a clue as to what has been done in Iraq by Americans; even the people in Iraq cannot grasp the misery the war (slaughter) has caused, in cosmic and fleshly terms. Imagine one Christmas light in 10,000 stuck in a bright strobe mode while all other lights are in dim light mode; the bright strobe will show up; indicating a problem that could affect other lights in the string. Likewise, Americans have to learn to discern the subtle and overt differences between Totalitarian methods of political control (of money and Human energy) in the name of democracy; as compared to ethical control (of money) with honest accounting democracy. (HINT: see how long it takes the police to haul you away for calling a police officer a liar when the police officer IS lying (under oath). If the majority of the people in a real democracy say "arrest congress and their families, and confiscate all their assets" then congress and their families must be arrested and their assets confiscated; that is, in a REAL democracy. In the current alleged democracy, ONLY congress could legislate such a law that would allow the arrest of congress, which of course congress will never do; so we need a revolution of some other kind; i.e. citizens arrest if that is legal. There is no law (yet) against intelligent revolution with non-violent intent. Congress is guilty of Treason, and the evidence is all in, it's just mislabeled and being overlooked for more important news, like another celebrity drug overdose or athlete in an assault, sex, cocaine, wife beating (and cheating) arrest case story book deal with huge tax potentials. You can be sure that if the majority of the people said "arrest congress," the National Guard would be put on red alert; you'd think Al Qaeda was here in person, in America, underground, setting up shop. Allegedly, American soldiers used to take a vow stating they would never take arms against Americans in civil disputes involving the government and citizens. The incidents at Kent State University and Waco compound put that falsehood to rest rather convincingly I do believe. In my opinion, both of the incidents, and others, could have been handled without a shot being fired. Although Rodney King was a man in trouble with his own thinking and behavior, he did not deserve the beating, O.J. Simpson is guilty, and George Bush, Dick Cheney, Donald Rumsfeld, Condo Rice, Bill Clinton, at least 1,500 judges and 20,000 lawyers and doctors each, coast to coast, and several other white collar CEO, banker, Wall Street, corporation president, super star athlete criminals, bums, etc. should all be arrested, in my opinion. Did you read the article on one of the great news wires about "the government being willing to help soldiers" who returned from a rock and e rack with some of the money needed to get their G.E.D.? Your government, giving young uneducated men and women guns and orders to go in a foreign land and start killing or be killed. Humans fighting over ancient beliefs relative to the economics of believing in a god, God, or GOD; or who's "god" is the most peace loving, and who's god offers the biggest rewards in the afterlife; is not smart, but we do it anyway. Then, we blame the victims of our attack for "our need" to be in their homeland; to protect ourselves from being attacked by them in our homeland. Actually, as we know now, current American leaders want a U.S. siphon in the oil well profit and tax money. This behavior is NOT Christian or Muslim behavior; it is typical immature vain rich kid greed monster political party personality type behavior on a large scale. Maybe everyone should have a college degree before being eligible to enlist in the armed forces. Of course the state would have to make a better than we have now college education program available to everyone. People often have a degree with no real knowledge about interacting with other people. Competing is easier than co-operating because deception is almost standard in all competitions; and educated people have been conditioned to expect being deceived about some part of everything where competition over money is involved. Have you ever had that feeling of: "so that is how they make their money on this deal! It just sounded "to free" to be profitable for anyone to be able to afford all the television advertising to practically give something away for FREE!" Free, and freedom are two of the most over used and abused words in our language; freedumb is an under used word (I made it up). Freedom isn't free, it is a weapon word in a tax, fee, and fine game of "mother may I" that is played with double talking rules where only one side of the debate can use guns, or lie under oath and not be punished.

Here is an out of place note, out of place to help you see and remember this FACT; technically, government employees do NOT pay income tax. Government employee "pay" IS the tax money non-government employees have already paid; the money just gets passed around (represented as numbers on pieces of paper until a government employee "gets their share" and cashes a payroll check for collecting and spending taxes other people have paid). Tax on tax is not new, it's democratic (in a negative way of deceiving the masses). Simply put, America needs new leadership, a true democratic leadership format; not in Fabian-socialist sub-format headed towards socialism like we have been in for more than 20 years now. To resolve a large part of the problem, new leaders are needed, not new republicans and new democrats who choose to "rise up" off their congressional thrones to "run" for a position of greater influence. I am tired of buying toilet paper for government employees, but setting up a "new" Political Party in America is an exceedingly difficult task, an expensive task, and not something that can be accomplished in a year (by one person). In most cases lawyers are needed for this, most of whom are republicans or democrats. However, if the endeavor is not for personal gain, no paid by the hour lawyer will be involved; especially to aid someone who wants to oppose "their" party affiliation. No American can afford to pay a lawyer what it would take to represent my friend's cases against the IRS; at least that is what the $250.00 per hour lawyers say. Lawyers will not hide the fact that few people win in a case against the law makers unless large sums are spent before trial ($50,000.00 up front retainer), and the violation or whatever is a flagrant violation of incompetence with neglect and reckless endangerment, and a multi-million dollar settlement is possible. Time is never or rarely pressing to a lawyer. America and the world needs freedom from the freedumb; republicans and democrats are doing more negative damage than positive re-positioning. The greatest job market might be in teaching and training the know and have nothings in the world how to learn and do something positive; like rebuild all of the "slums" of the world and clean up our planet while we still have time. Instead of spending the money overseas rebuilding what we destroy, lets not spend any more money destroying things (which would prevent spending re-building money AND save a lot of people from a lot of misery and death), arm our citizens with jobs, confidence, security, and support, and clean up and rebuild our country. People are a lot like molecules.

All molecules exist in their own space and time. This life is made possible by particles in the outflow of the molecules that are by-products of future time and space. One thing is certain, "things" have to get better, or we will self destruct (more than half the population killed). Don't worry though, the universe can retrieve anything that existed any time in the universe (I will say this again, a sound bite that needs to be heard). The world is just not safe in its current state, and Humans made the world unsafe in a large part, as a matter of free will. Like the atoms in anything, Human life exists in its own space and time. Earth is a testing facility. The atoms in the Human life giving brain energy wave field are less than one fourth of a tea spoon; in a molecular soup the size of the universe. Again, the universe never loses anything, and can recover anything that was suspected of being lost; even quantities less than a tea spoon. The universe controls all access to time and space, and allows just about anything we can imagine. Allowing is different than condoning. Humans have repetitive problems in managing Human behavior. Humans cannot see what is hiding in the light that gives us the ability to see, feel, think, and perceive life. But we can see that beautiful woman who needs and wants some attention right away. All that is allowed is not also approved, and evidently the lesson here is a very great lesson that has to be learned if Humans are interested in staying alive. If I could see with the eyes of the universe, I believe I would not like too much of what I see on planet "Earth" relative to Human interaction over sex and money (which includes religion, the law, advertising, sports, "the news," etc.).

We are all travelling down the same Human road alright, but some of us are turning this planet of Human life into a dump or hell for everyone other than "their own kind." In this case, "their own kind" is simply "the king and his courts, his police, and supporters;" meaning alleged "service" organizations (bureaucrats, "experts," lobbyists) and or "the paper pusher people" midway up on the money heap with guns and self granted immunity "to get" the money FOR the "higher ups" (i.e. congress, presidents, military, political parties). To me, it is sad that some people are "American proud" to be slaves, still today in 2009, who, even in total desperation, reproduce and perpetuate their own desperation, waving a flag, hoping that "their child" will have a better life. America's two political parties are like two gangs. As long as the people in the opposing gangs throw the same rocks back and forth at each other in support of their religious gang land bible credo beliefs relative to their conservative or liberal political beliefs, there will be blood and chaos in everything. The key words here are "same rocks," "religious gang," "conservative or liberal," "the people," and "blood and chaos."

Although every business "entity" has its own cyclical economy, we are all part of a bigger economy, so we really only have one gigantic economy made up of many smaller economies. The current U.S. government leadership direction is towards a pseudo-democratic socialistic Totalitarian government headed towards all out Communism, or a one world government and economic system. Face it, admit it, and realize it, the building blocks are everywhere. What are American, Asian, European, South and Central American, and other countries (governments and "international corporations") working towards? Ways to turn the individual markets into ONE global market? Make no mistakes; capitalist greed and military preparedness mean a lot in international negotiations over ways to create jobs and enslave the masses with tax programs. One global money market will have to have one set of accepted international laws. In my professional, up close, in your face experience in the legal world, every effort has to be made to cut out over half of the legal fees in everything, which is mostly paper pushing anyway. The real, Majority of the Human population has to be in control of "the law" AND "THE MONEY;" NOT an alleged majority of the "representatives" who really are not representatives except unto themselves and the lobbyist with the most money, gifts, and best cover; i.e. oil companies, drug makers, car companies, etc.

The world is not going to surrender or succumb to the ideals, laws, methods, leadership, practices, etc. of any unaltered current version of the politically corrupt (Totalitarian Fabian Socialist almost a police state) American Way; with leaders who profess democratic process. I have been to foreign countries, and I know what many foreigners think of America. We kill more of our own than any nation in the history of the world, we're number one alright; in the killing of our own category (excluding abortion). No doubt, don't get me wrong, I do not want to live in most of the other countries in the world, I'm just trying to start an international conversation for a one world democratic government with democratically socialist elements. If crime can be reduced 50%, the cost of fighting crime will have to go down. My goal would be to eliminate crime at the source; the attitude of every individual. A 100% eradication of all crime is probably out of the question, sadly. Freedumb is not the same as freedom. Energy production, health care, insurance, car production, water and natural gas utilities, banks, and some other businesses should be socialized to a large extent. Multi-million dollar bonuses and stock option benefits have to end. Yes, some of us Americans have proud public (cosmic and international) sex and drug addiction problems, our political system is almost a farce, our legal system works once in a while but is primarily a cash cow for lawyers and their staffs. Yes, I know, we're still not "as bad" as some places, I know, I've heard it, I've seen it firsthand. But we could be a lot better. Some people want a war right here in the city streets of America because of past blunders made by people who lived more than one hundred years ago; not smart at all. Americans are in denial about the truth in many things that affect everyone. Historically speaking, America fits the pattern of a nation headed for a disaster. America will probably come out of this current situation, learn a great deal of valuable information, then go through another set of ups and downs before America becomes much more European and Asian. Maybe not. I am sick of Americans telling me to be satisfied with mediocrity.

Life's temporary stages are simply the result of molecules behaving in time and space, according to "laws of the universe" that are at this time a mystery to everyone who lives in this dimension. The properties of molecules we donate to the universal soup will determine where we emerge in the slurry in our next life; or so it seems to some from a molecular perspective. It seems the universe wants to expedite refinement of everything as quickly as possible, but there is no hurry. We move through the common invisible electromagnetic transport zone as quickly as the laws of the invisible will allow. Part of the problem in our life is that too few of us share in the pleasure associated with the end result of our own work. In my yet to emerge into world, the one in my electrical pathway, no one suffers over money, there is no waste of any kind, music comes out of the air, everything smells like fresh flowers, the girls taste like mint candy, pain, poverty, worry, lust, jealousy, crime, and hate do not exist, work is like play and getting dirty is impossible. Warm and cool, flowing, pleasant smelling, drinkable water is everywhere. Everyone will LOVE their work, and every need of everyone will be met. In our current state, the universe will help us (release knowledge leading to new technology) IF we demonstrate a willingness to change our negative ways, i.e. warring over money, mineral wealth, sex, oil, gas, religion, ceremony, taxes, words, lies, ancient history, sports scores, etc.

In a real democratic socialist society (with all the crap cut out) children of all ages would LOVE school, and everyone would LOVE life. At age 16, when children are more advanced than school children of the same age today, as part of their education, they will work and study, being paid a fair wage; say $15,000.00 per year. This money will be managed by banks, mostly going towards college; a portion for retirement, and a little for fun. At age 17, the wage goes up to $16,000.00, and so on; age 18, wage goes up to $17,000.00 until six years of college are completed. Starting in high school, children go to school seven months, work for three months and have two months of vacation. Children will LOVE to work and study. By this time, every student has the equivalent of a master's degree in two different disciplines; plus a minor. The job market will be wide open. (This is more clearly explained in another document I will tell you about later). As adults, we work seven months, have three months of job training, further education, and job skill improvement training; and two months of vacation. We all job share, and there is always 100% employment.

For your further information I have made over a million dollars with my hands and with no one's help. In the last 16 years, I have done a lot of free work for good customers and friends, and have under charged as much or more, and still made a better than average income. I did all the bleeding, all the driving, all the risking, all the scheduling, all the accounting, and all of the labor myself. My Spouse could support herself without me, and she also works with her hands and her mind. I am thankful, deeply; that my customers allowed me to do my money making thing, and that they have said so many good things about me. Due to injuries from a five (5) car auto accident, (NOT my fault) I can only work three and a half days per week instead of the regular six (6) days a week. Since the time of the accident, my income has been cut in half, aided by the economics, ethics, and integrity of America's 2006-2010 downturn. A revolution of a new type is in the horizon. The same old American ways are going to change.

The current slow changing American government system is clearly a Totalitarian Fabian Socialist (centralized autocratic rule with force and a facade of democracy that moves slowly into socialism) police state, and a pseudo democratic Ponzi Mafia IRS money scamming war mongering dictatorship. Moralistic ethics are gone; the best we can get today is lip service ethics that are void of common sense, and often totally lacking honesty. Greed driven denial has replaced morals in ethical issues. One lawyer I hired told me "Al, the American court system is a crap chute, and the plea agreement is the Drano that keeps the court process flowing." This lawyer was a former deputy prosecutor in a large U.S. city (used his title to pick up women, had no real interest in fairness in the law, and turned out to be thoroughly lacking integrity; replaced it with vanity and arrogance).

"Marshall law," or American police and military personnel in large numbers roaming the streets of America with shoot to kill orders is not as far fetched as it sounds, and it could happen in a matter of minutes. Maybe then Americans might think twice before trying to steal someone else' s car, truck, boat, stereo, tools, jewelry, furniture, art, guns, cash, food, child, or motorcycle; or molest someone else's or their own child, or rape someone, male or female; or do some other stupid thing. Freedumb is everywhere freedom allegedly exists; and way too often, scum bag criminals have more rights than law abiding citizens, in way too many cases; as a matter of "the law." Again, idiots for judges and lawyers and congressmen and women. Allegedly the law exists to protect innocent people (who work and pay taxes and seek to improve their position in life without harming others) who obey the law. Any act that infringes on the simple rights of individuals needs to be addressed by everyone. In my personal opinion, American television is freedumb stupid. We can't wait for one dead man (murdered by "the government" in his time) to "come back and save us" from stupid use of our own individual free will. We do not need violence to take control of our government, the government needs violence to stay in control. Stop. Change of subject.

Personally, I m all for getting the toilet and everything about the toilet OFF the television or solely on "The toilet channel." Everything and more that anyone wants or needs to know about the toilet and human waste management would be on the toilet channel. Maybe every child needs 50 hours of "The toilet channel" as training in grade school, then we can see if toilets get any cleaner in America. As I may have said earlier, as instructed to say by my friend's Spouse, I am also for putting all commercials on individual subject area channels based on categories; i.e. prescription drugs, insurance, cars, fast food, soft drinks, etc. each have their own channel. Regular movie, sports, science, comedy, talk, and other programming never gets interrupted for ANY commercials, and only for viewer pit stops and snack grabbing breaks. Pre-selected music will play during breaks. People NEED a break from pathetic commercials and loud mouthed announcers.

Yes, "the government" has a huge annual toilet paper budget, and "the government" makes a lot of money in taxes from the advertising industry, but most big corporations do not pay taxes on everything like end of the line consumers. Don't fool yourself though, large and small corporations pay staggering amounts in taxes on a regular basis, but also get huge breaks, and can bend the law to extremes. For example, how could there ever be an accurate audit of General Motors? What an open door for corruption; with all the facets of that operation, CEO "bonuses" is not all that is going out the door in large quantities. And all this lying about MONEY; too few people have too much, and a large portion of the population who needs more money, would waste most or all of any gift money they might receive as fast as they got it if it were "just given" to them. I work for my money. My parents lived in a trailer when I was born, I came from a position of poverty, and today I am better off than most (a result of hard work), and live a comfortable, quiet, low key, modest lifestyle, on the edge of constant change. Recall the FACT that new republicans and democrats is NOT new change in leadership; republicans are still republicans and democrats are still democrats. I jump around with subjects as a psychological tool to try and help you remember certain things; just wanted you to know that.

Face it, people can be fools when it comes to money, tradition, religion, politics, ceremony, public alcohol related events, sex, sports, vanity, taxes, and just about anything. The people who are the government are first and foremost interested in having a job tomorrow. Clearly, the "job of the government" is not to establish fairness, peace, and a method to help all people live happy lives, but rather to make sure the people rarely get what they want; i.e. true freedom, prosperity, equality, justice for all, peace, common sense laws, security from war, safety from local and international crime, truth and common sense in spending, honesty, real education and not slave training and brainwashing, and the like. Monuments, parks, street lights, streets, and signs are needed, but people pay too much for such things for the "service" they provide, economically. Roads, street signs, street lights, and "emergency crews" do not make peace. "The government" (people) wastes billions in quadruplicate paper work processing, postage, copy paper, telephone, toilet, computer expenses, office supplies, etc. alone every year (tax money) that with the money wasted, half of America could be fed (every year). The important words here are "government" "people" "wastes" "tax money" "every year" "America."

From a worker slave position, I know life is borderline worthless if there is not some money left over from the weekly paycheck AFTER all living expenses and taxes are paid. "It's still better than living in China" is NOT a good enough reason to NOT fix the problem (too few people have too much money and money is too hard to keep). Just barely able to pay the bills is a poor foundation for starting a family (reproducing the struggle to pay the bills). Americans have learned how to disrespect life in favor of pursuing money. Americans have also learned how to disrespect life in favor of pursuing self glorification. Respect cannot exist in any two way relationship where one person must first adhere unquestionably with the philosophy of the other party or parties "in the relationship" as if the "enforcement" of the "relationship agreement" would "be fair, unbiased, not prejudiced, and ethical with a commonly accepted moral foundation" (that in fine print also includes murdering opponents to the belief system as directed by the leaders of the group enforcing the agreement). The key words are "adhere with the philosophy of the other party without question" (even though you do not know all of the whole philosophy, like the part where you agreed to kill in order to perpetuate the philosophy of the group, or be killed by the group in order to ensure the protection of the privacy and identity of the group members).

We, the people who can read this, are simply one form of being in this life environment. Simple. All of us are a lot alike; however, some of us use this common set of factors "against" others; as in "everything you say can and will BE USED AGAINST YOU." "I am innocent" "I am not guilty" "I am telling the truth" "You have the wrong person" are statements that can "be used AGAINST" the speaker; even if the truth is being told. Brain power does not have a skin color. All skin color groups have diversity in personality type. Personality type super cedes all other things in Human behavior. Innocence and guilt often comes down to a personality type issue; a perception, judgment, and learned bias matter, not a complete truth, morality, or ethical concern. Everyone is born with the potential to be any of the definable, naturally occuring 16 Jungian personality types (combinations of Introvert, Extravert, Sensor, Intuitive, Thinker, Feeler, Judger, Perceiver) and any one of many Greek archetypes (such as but not limited to engineer, doctor, athlete, sage, warrior, artist, thief, cook, mother, father, guardian, craftsman), which is the footer for the foundation of expression for the active personality type. Unconsciously, our natural lesser used preferences for perception and judgment create a "shadow" character, and we seek a balance in our environments (and use of perception and judgment) by adjusting our priorities to target our goals with greater accuracy, in time. Priorities are like invisible plans that outline patterns of behavior through which we self direct our energy in time toward reaching an objective and completion of a larger goal (I choose to spend my time doing this instead of that). Priorities in every life are influenced by genetics, peers, environments, parents behavior, certain events, personal experience, etc. Sorry, but I see an America that is a priority scatter brain society. Everyone in America SHOULD be rich and comfortable by now, but we are a LONG way from that position. Americans are largely pre-occupied with "how do I get the money" "get noticed" "get a girl" "get a guy" "the right job" or the this-and-that so I can do the other things I prefer to be doing when I find some time. We the people in the world today seem to want ONE common goal for Humanity that encompasses everything we do. In simple terms "be rich, safe, secure, have fun, no pain" are some common objectives, but we are stuck in the struggle to have it all like a CD stuck on one line of a song, and we keep playing the same old "fight" song every time we come to a crossroads; where very few make it through the intersection towards greater success. Our national motto could change from a fight base to an educate base. Democratic socialism is not as bad as what is alleged. We have a form of democratic socialism right now that is neither a hybrid democratic or socialist "government." I do not have a clue about the current president's (2009-2010) definition of democratic socialism; or the world's interpretation of the limited knowledge used to define the current (and every other) Totalitarian generated economic downturn for the masses.

Market correction really means profit taking session. Some people drink wine and champagne and eat lobster regularly while others die of starvation, insane violence, preventable disease, avoidable accidents, and abortion. Okay, so the richest billionaires lost two of fifty billion, millions of Humans in America are struggling, killing, and stealing their ways to survival $20.00 at a time, hundreds of thousands or a couple million or more Americans are white collar criminals, and at last count, America has more people in prison than any nation, and the struggle continues. Humans really could solve most if not all of their own (self created) problems. Government is an obstacle to freedom, in the current state anyway.

Humans are like a satellite signal receiver with a neglected maintenance need and a corroded connection. We as a species are failing to keep our channels open to the source of our future; as if the universe would reject its own creation. We as a species have discovered how to put huge nuclear bomb launching devices hundreds of miles up in the atmosphere with digital micro-chip and laser communication, triggering, steering, and navigation equipment, but we can't realize what we are fighting over. Real estate and limited space location? Time and money? Or just plain old stupid Human free will behavior; and pride? Surely there is a place that is just as "holy" on Earth as Israel is supposed to be. Actually, in spiritual molecular reality, the entire planet is "holy" or NONE of it is. If the fine people of Israel were truly interested in world peace, they would move out of what is called Israel. The "holy land" will still be there, Biblically speaking, even if the Jews move out. If "GOD's will is going to be done," does it matter who lives where? NO. Surely there is a location on planet Earth where a new Israel could be established. Kida is a Jewish name, I know, I'm Jewish. Being that all land is holy, wherever the Jewish nation starts over, the land will be holy. All land belongs to the universe, not to Humans. "Some people" charge others a property tax; like the "some people" own the Earth and have a right to charge people to live on Earth. "We" need intelligent, honest leaders who cannot be corrupted with money, recognition, and a lax legal system run by other criminal politicians.

"We need that property tax money to pay for the schools so we can educate the people" the politicians claim. But let's consider this; the "education" is actually programmed propaganda to train and teach people to become programmed taxpayer slaves. Government run education was first a subject in the writings of spiritual philosophers over 4,000 years ago when the infamous Lao Tzu said "government run education perpetuates ignorance." (Lao Tzu was a teacher of Kung Fu Tzu, or Confucius; who together developed and spread the "Yin Yang" philosophy, the use of Tai Chi, and "Kung Fu," (which is originally based in spiritual study and self defense, and is the base of what has become "mixed martial arts;" which is a misuse of the art in spiritual terms). The point is, there will always be "some people" who are more willing to start a fight to get what they want instead of earning the money to buy what they want; or by making it their self.

What more proof does anyone need to know that something MUCH greater than the Human mind HAS TO EXIST in dimensions of space and time we cannot see? To that form of a being do I pledge allegiance, not to a government that does what any government on Earth does today; as in dictate taxation with military force, stupidity, and economic measures; i.e. interest rates, application fees, license fees, Medicare fraud, seat belt laws, retirement account restrictions and fees, foreign wars in Iraq, Iran, Afghanistan, India, Pakistan; and the local U.S. government and police verses the U.S. masses over taxes war.

With this in mind, consider this "other dimension" definition of the word "patriotism,"(which is an intangible mental position, a mental "stance or pose" that typically plays out in war activity). Just relax, read, and think "higher knowledge": PATRIOTISM: 1). the outspoken faith and psychological worship of a man made set of standards and beliefs as a foundation for an alleged application of philosophical principles and actions in a social, economic, militarized, or politically religious legal system that preaches peace and practices war at the same time, and in the name of an invisible being, i.e. a Patriot for a country (being "willing to kill and be killed" over Human made symbolism and false claims of a superior government system of Humans); 2) PATRIOTIC behavior has a "faith" factor, as in faith in an alleged "prophet of GOD" who teaches nonviolence and forgives for violence, as in a "God AND Country" philosophical position for PATRIOTISM, which is a psychological gimmick that helps people brainwash themselves into believing that "the creator of the universe WANTS us to kill all the people who oppose OUR form of democracy" 3) Patriots perpetuate and protect the philosophy and practices of the government who taxes the masses and gives part of the money to the soldiers. (The job of every soldier is to protect the people who collect the taxes and pay the soldiers); 4). the job of a patriotic soldier includes having and demonstrating unquestioned belief in what is preached by the commanding officers and congress (the same as voluntarily being a self brainwashed robot for people who will kill over money, gas, oil, the sound of words in a free speech dialogue, Truths that expose government corruption, a traffic ticket, virtually anything a soldier or cop wants to do is fair play, even venting personal marital problems on unsuspecting innocent drivers in a traffic stop); 5) Patriotism also includes a willingness to sacrifice your entire family based on what "some people" say about their alleged motivations for creating four new taxes to pay for another war; 6) Patriotism also includes a willingness to kill the family of those whose oppose a particular free will choice belief system; 7). Patriotic behavior goes FAR beyond voting for liars and the lesser of two evils, chanting clichés, carrying signs, marching, quoting ancient Human Bible scripture, and professing a biased political preference by a party name.

Regardless, killing in 2009 over something someone may have said 2,000 or more years ago is insane. Reproducing unproductive sources of potential (people who do not want to get an education or learn a skill or trade or profession and work) is socially self destructive. Uneducated people are more likely to become criminals than educated people, but a lot of education is nothing but slave training, and there are a lot of educated stupid people in positions of great influence who are criminals. Anyway we look at it, uneducated people are a burden to educated people, and are also a source of income for a lot of semi-educated people who know how to manipulate uneducated and educated people to get to their money.

Some patriotic people can be and are criminals and victims of other patriotic people's negative behavior. Patriotism has good and bad characteristics, as in "if" the government is corrupt and you still support the corrupt people who are the government, you are guilty of everything they do that is negative in the "eyes of the universe." The universe is fully 100% aware of everything everyone does; the video camera of the universe is on all the time. Everyone's life can be reviewed, which happens when our molecular signature is scrutinized by the universe, probably by the second, but surely at the transformation process time (this existence to the next; not death, but transformation). I rest humbly on a belief that is founded in the manners in which this existence re-cycles itself. I can only hope the universe will do what my friend Mr. Freije is hoping for; i.e. examine the molecular signature of my life and find that I meet the requirements to live in a world much like this one, but with NO need for a toilet, a landfill, or that has any form of waste, decay, smoke, foul odor, infectious bacteria, dirty anything, hate, violence, or anything we call criminal activity in America (that the courts allow anyway if tax revenue can be collected and people can be accepted into an environment where they and others can more easily get arrested for being drunk, free, and behaving unacceptably). My and your getting arrested (traffic ticket, whatever) generates personal income for police, lawyers, and government employees in the courts. Something like the prohibition of alcohol and marijuana generates billions in revenue for police, lawyers, and government employees in the courts every year. Legalizing marijuana and going after the abusers of alcohol and meth users and makers will IMPROVE many things in America. If people would act democratically, Americans and the world population of slaves could work together and end all poverty and stupidity, and Humans could re-build all we have damaged (most of it anyway); and get on a new path to prevent major setbacks from occurring via the political or religious systems. Most flower gardens need regular maintenance (weed pulling sessions).

It is not just people in foreign nations who are "mad" at the U.S. "government;" people in America are mad at the U.S. government. Americans are also mad at the U.S. media, and U.S. court system, and U.S. education system, and U.S. church organizations, and the U.S. congress, the IRS, U.S. president, U.S. speaker of the house, the U.S. military, and the former three U.S. administrations. In reality, the biggest burden to the American people (a huge cancerous tumor) is the group of people who are the United States government, starting at the top with congress (presidents are cute show puppets for congress). The majority of the American people DO NOT "rule" or "control" anything in America other than their own complacency and fear of their "church going" leaders, who expect to be respected for "going to church." Everyone is responsible for 100% of their free will behavior.

What we need, in my terroristic opinion is co-operation, not more violence. I am a Peace activist terrorist; U.S. government employees hate me for being peaceful; which is not really American you know. There has to be a job for everyone, and if everyone will work, there should not be poverty ANYWHERE. Selling "education based laborers" to foreign nations (by request only) to help improve living conditions in overpopulated poverty stricken areas (not passing out free milk and bread) is a great way to make friends (WORKING with people, not stealing from them). The Earth is filthy compared to before "modernization," and a job in environmental cleanup would be a delight compared to flipping dead animal flesh burgers in a fast food restaurant, for a lot of people anyway. After America has been rebuilt, all poverty gone, THEN we offer our assistance, but we need to clean up our act FIRST. We cannot afford to turn America into Africa (starving, sick, weak, diseased, uneducated, "hopeless without help" masses under the leadership of corrupt governments), and we have a moral, ethical, universal obligation to offer assistance; AFTER helping Americans FIRST. However, we cannot cram everything about our lifestyle down the throats of children and adults seeking improvement in their standard of living. Primitive men "gang banged" little girls in all of their primitive lines, and America's porn often brings primitive ignorance into modern times as if to say, "see, we haven't changed all that much!" My Spouse and I have been married over 26 years, so we are what most would say is mature in that area; not boring, mature. Outside of our house, like in politics and religion, sex based ignorance is everywhere and growing in popularity, and is out of control. Americans are simply stupid about sex. I am convinced we are better off if we keep the sex under better cover, and that we grow up. Let's become independently financially secure on your own before we reproduce a clone of our flesh. America is suffering from the current high level of abusive one way negative result freedumb "some people" are allowed to use by law to make money (such as creating taxes, fines, and fees to levy on the people; fish in an upcoming example) to pay the people who process the paperwork associated with collecting fines, fees, and taxes, of which millions are collected, and the court operates at a loss on paper. Human Parasites, baby mentality Humans in adult Human bodies, most government employees. The "we are in control" attitude with "mother may I like rules" to collect your money (with fines, fees, interest, and taxes) "to buy food to feed OUR KIDS!!!" is a pure Totalitarian form of behavior, especially when deputies free willfully commit perjury in court (like in Johnson County Indiana, hi guys, you liars). A good example of defective "government employees" abusing people for money is with traffic tickets costing hundreds of dollars. I am sensitive about driving because I see so much pathetic behavior by drivers, almost every day, and all day when I am on the road. For every driver who gets a ticket, 1,000 or more drivers per minute who deserve a ticket do not get a ticket. Everyone who gets a ticket does not deserve a ticket for whatever they did or did not do (AND say "mother may I") at the time of getting a ticket. Instead, traffic ticket writing is like a flock of 200 birds fishing in the ocean (hovering and diving in from over 50-100 feet up) over a school of desirable fish with numbers in the hundreds of thousands (kind of hard to miss a target). How many traffic tickets (fish) does a city police force have to write (catch) to pay the overheard for one day (to support a group of people who contribute NOTHING, but have the right to spend your future, or pull you over in broad daylight and ROB you with an ink pen, badge, gun, salary, computer and video equipment)? Freedumb has replaced a lot of the common sense with basic respect "freedom" that America used to allegedly represent in the world, along with honesty, ethics, sobriety, integrity, yea, we've heard it all, I know. Respect is the key word here. You may not like what he or she does, but if it is in private, and NO ONE suffers (and both people are willing and eager) then let them do whatever it is if they keep it private, and mind your own business; respect their privacy. I know it is hard sometimes, the law can't and won't help, so I just tell myself, "as long they don't touch you with it, all you can do is leave the area of the source of the conflict, or learn to live with being annoyed;"(which is a form of suffering). At the same time, I am tired of paying insurance premiums to pay for things people could prevent on a large scale; i.e. heart failure due to poor diet, HIV/AIDS, obesity, diabetes, medical malpractice, unplanned and unwanted pregnancy, smoking meth, too much alcohol, driving accidents, etc.). Capitalism.

Capitalism is out of control, it is not evil in itself, just out of control. Some of the big players in the capitalist markets are out of touch with the people who do the dirty work that becomes their wealth; isn't that right Wall Street? A lot of the money made on Wall Street goes down the toilet, down the urinal, up the nose, in the vein, in the pipe, to the condom companies, for overpriced rent, insurance, etc. We live in a socialist state where some people pay for the everything everyone else needs, wants and uses. The high cost of Wall Street living is built into the price I pay to have my money "invested," which also means "stolen." We have the super rich who have more than enough of everything, the hands out genetically damaged impoverished masses, and the struggling abused workers trapped in between. America and the world needs to use a little more common sense in everything, as in sharing the wealth, information and knowledge. What people do not know IS suppressing and restraining Human potential in general. Legislating "new laws" that are directed at EVERYONE but only affect a few (the "see what we can do to you" attitude) is like releasing a deadly virus in a rural area "to see" what happens (create work for government employees, generate taxes in the private sector, make some people very ill, perhaps kill some people, alter genetics for the next generation of affected individuals, create new fears of terrorism, spend large sums of tax dollars to pay investigators to study the messy matter, and if the answer is discovered, spend more tens of thousands or millions of dollars talking about and deciding how to cover the matter up, how to prevent lawsuits, deny all true facts, and hopefully forever silence all talk of the many deaths and illnesses). Universally fair enforcement of all laws has to become a priority if any society is going to survive, but first, we need new laws in many cases. The many can no longer trust the few to "do what is best" for everyone; a new democracy has to take over, peacefully, I hope. Admit it ladies and gentlemen, our democracy is broken, and corruption is the rust that ate the foundation. Every issue affecting Humans via the government needs to be "broken down" into the smallest components so everyone can see why things are the way they are at present; which should lead to better ways in the future to do the same thing. The "some, many people who are the government" do not want any improvements in anything until they "cut themselves in" with some form of tax. The on the clock "pay time" to "pay" government employees to talk about "the issues" and "how much" the tax increase will be, drags on and on, sometimes for years. Who would try to deny that congress waste billions every year?

In other words, each and every "Human issue" needs to be voted on by the people, not **alleged** "representatives" of the people who turn out to be biased for the large corporations who employ the most people (more tax at one location, and easier record keeping in most cases, etc.). Capitalism itself is not evil, but some Humans (congress, CEO's, etc.) have made capitalism evil where it is evil. Capitalism is NOT democracy or socialism, and capitalism is not religious. Capitalism is immature, spiritually. Forms of negative capitalism (deception) exist everywhere. What was once "fair," friendly, progressive, capitalism; has turned into extreme greed bloodletting and destruction with war capitalism. Our "group freedumb" has helped 90% of us realize that defensive positioning in our asset diversification is essential for short and long term security. Finding (honest) competent "money changers" (broker/dealers, financial advisors, etc.) is a treacherous endeavor. I am tired of looking at another down side crisis of another up and down capitalist profit taking session (huge profits for a few insiders at Wall Street), which is a crisis for the majority of the investors. There are better ways of life than this struggling over money and sex commercial advertising insanity. We all need a break from it, beginning about now. America cannot force the rest of the world to surrender to the American plan for a one world government and one world economy that is a mirror image of America, in the current state. What do you think our leaders (in 2009) mean when they speak of "positioning America for the world economy" or "the international marketplace?" The EXACT type of system we have here in America is really what? (hint: militarized Totalitarian capitalist). "Democratic republic" and "a democracy;" are two misnomers relative to accurately describing America's corrupt government. If you cannot see that the current and past few White House regimes have convincingly demonstrated that America is in a state of FLAWED functioning, your thinking is flawed, perhaps too many roots in the layer of dark heavy sludge in the universal slurry of molecular energy. The media would have everyone believe that America has a functioning democracy, but that is simply ludicrous. Democracy died years ago. Look at and listen to the news, all U.S. government leadership and dollar based economic direction is focused on "one world" economics and military control. There was an ancient America, only it was called Phrygia, where Turkey is today, where the Hittites once ruled. Phrygia and America are two peas in a pod, except Phrygia was primitive and was overrun, caught off guard by an enemy they could have defeated with ease on the battlefield. When the Cimmerians invaded Phrygia during the great Phrygian annual religious celebration period, "the church and state" became two separate organizations in many ways; and here we are, America, on the verge of what could become a civil war, like in the former Soviet Union. As we also know, other nations ARE planning to attack America. Our demoncratic laws allow foreign terrorists to legally immigrate into America (or visit and get lost in the paperwork) and set up bomb making classes while you are getting a ticket for "not wearing your seat belt properly!" In 2007, IRS employees gave away over $2.7 BILLION in fraudulent refunds (inside IRS employees creating excessive refunds to a "network" of family members, etc.; there ARE many other IRS embezzling, stealing, forging, and other fraudulent activities recorded in the official record of the tax inspector general). In 2008, Medicare ONLY "gave away" $98,000,000,000.00 in FRAUDULENT claim payments!!!). America's alleged democratic government (that is run, operated, and ruined by a minority), gives away and wastes MORE money every year than it would take to make everyone in America a millionaire. I do not believe that everyone deserves to be a millionaire in the present state of America, but I do believe that everything broken can be fixed or replaced. I have no respect for competitive deception, which is a foundation for abusive capitalism, as in banking, the stock market, insurance, medical practice, legal field (giant pig pen), sports, the automotive industries, and MOST other capitalistic businesses.

I believe Humans should be able to engage in any type of harmless activity they desire, but a lot of what we Americans have put on our satellites in high definition (porno for example), uh, do you, we; REALLY want "beings" with greater than our own technology seeing what SOME of us "love" to make the focus of "our life energy?" Talk about showing (the unknown potential enemy) our Human weakness, television and porn does it in style (and the commercials, sitcoms, talk shows, news; we need to stand back and take of good look and refocus). I also believe everyone needs to be elevated to a cleaner, more productive and relaxed level than the current "standard of living" level for about 35% of the population. To me, even though I think college has gone "capitalist" (money crazy) instead of really striving to be a foundation of EDUCATION, there is no reason why America should not have a 100% college educated, employed population. Further, like my "guru," I also believe that the Human existence is a by-product of a naturally occurring, pre-programmed, chemical process. This unique stage of life seems to be a "processing" dimension that is used by the universe to refine the microscopic pieces (less than half a teaspoon of highly specialized particles) of the infinite power that exists in everything. This power moves on its own, is concentrated to a density Humans cannot calculate, is lighter than air, and is what is looking through our Human eyes. This unique group of molecules is what keeps our brains alive, our hearts beating, diaphragm moving, stomach churning, etc. The universe is using "our" bodies as collection devices to gather information that is beamed into the universal network of electro magnetism. Consider that this entire existence is a diverse conglomeration of particles behaving in the limits of "cosmic laws" we cannot understand as Humans. The cosmic laws work in such a way that we are allowed to perceive a minute display of the wide array of "the things" molecules can be used to make; i.e. the nuclear material that is our essence. I am getting ready to tell you where we get the words god, God, and GOD. As I said, I am not religious (a practitioner of ancient, traditional, ceremonial, rituals and obsessive compulsive neurotic behaviors). "IT" in the primitive Stoic philosophy is the "Generator, Operator, Destroyer" or GOD (not really primitive if you knew the sources, but dating back over 2,000 B.C.). God is a Human made political God, a Roman use of the word; and god is a pagan carved rock, a golden calf, a giant diamond, the original maker of wine (Dionysus, a Phrygian god), Cybele, the Human primitive (a Phrygian goddess also called Kubaba), "The Mother" of primitive Anatolian peoples ((modern Turkey)), who became the "Magna Mater" of the Roman Empire, and the "Mother of GOD" to other groups) and who "controlled" the use of "the food of the GODS," (hallucinogenic mushrooms and wheat fungus) for tribal leaders in orgy fest ceremonies. Zeus came out of the sex based intoxicated religion stage of Human development with the biggest name at the time, but was later discovered to be a fraud. Zeus had many children by many different women, and Zeus made his image largely from the work of Tantalus, the Phrygian King who was responsible for a lot of what happened in ancient Greece; i.e. ancient pharmacology, lotteries, gold refinement, the foundation for democracy, the study of individual behavior, and more. Zeus and Tantalus were very close friends, and Zeus betrayed Tantalus (falsely accused him of murdering his own son and stealing from the lottery and tax pool) in front of a council of leaders from surrounding nations (more like counties in primitive times), and the world has been under the control of the Zeus personality type ever since. Tantalus did not kill his son (Pelops, as in ruler of the Peloponnese, or Greek Islands, a primitive United Nations that included Phrygians, Minoans, Phoenicians, Ionians, Dorians, Macedonians, Sumerians, Athenians, Spartans, Thracians, and others). The Phrygians were the most renowned slave trade dealers, the "nation" with the greatest gross national combined product and services production in primitive times, for a while. Without Phrygian protection, the Hebrews and Armenians would have been wiped out long ago. The Phrygians gave refuge to troubled groups, helped them develop, and made them tax payer slaves where possible.

Most people seem to understand that our American social system and everything in it, like the meaning of words, is open to total corruption. When money is directly involved in a competitive with deception allowed arena, everybody wants in the game. In auto racing in the 1960's, an unspoken chunk of common knowledge was "cheaters win because they have the money to cheat and not get caught." Unfortunately, it seems that most American people do not realize that "government employee salaries and benefits, and WAR;" are the number one and two priorities of congress. The "we'll take your money and pay ourselves to tell you what to do," attitude is sickening and outdated. The "if you don't like the result, it's your fault because you elected us" attitude is even more disgusting. The worst attitude sounds like "love it or leave it;" depending on how you define "it." In summary then, it is clear that the current congress of the United States is pathetic, sickening, and outdated. By eliminating most of the negative, deceptive, anti-freedom decisions that congress makes (freedumb), all Americans could be millionaires in one year, if we cut our waste in half and redistributed the money in exchange for commitments not defined herein. I am opposed to giving money away to people who cannot manage what they have, or what they take from others, i.e. people who are the government. I prefer a mixed bag of resolution measures. One part is to arrest certain people and get some of the recovery money from them. I hate to say it, the rich and super rich have become super rich by taking advantage of an already advantageous situation (self made in some cases with hard work) where there is little competition (costs too much to get into the arena). Many rich people get rich by manipulating a large portion of what becomes their wealth away from less fortunate, or talented people. I suggest we put a cap on individual assets at $200 million dollars, which no one needs, ever, to be happy and content. The "need" for anything more is evidence of a psychiatric condition. With $200 million, anyone should be able to live the rest of their life from the interest. If such people want to work, okay, but you have to give all the new money away. Most of us just accept the money struggle as part of life, when in fact, money struggling is a Human made situation. This must change if the world wants to get out of this layer in the cosmic slurry. We all need relief from the money demand pressure, and the egomaniac elements involved.

No religion, skin color, gender group, or political party has ever solved any moral problem in the world, like for example, pagan god worship rituals involving Human sacrificial murder, or abortion, which is a primitive practice and is not new at all. There are still deep in the jungle voodoo murder practices, there is "super weirdo" internet and video stuff that is legal, so it is safe for me to say the world is mostly immoral and savage with symbols of potential toward real, modern civilization. Humans have been "performing" abortions for thousands of years." Think about this fact, abortions have been "performed" (like a ballet?) for thousands of years. Who came up with the term "perform" an "abortion" as if such an action has artistic attributes? A female abortion performance artist? Abortionist Art School. America's one world everything has a sex problem swimming in a pool of international blood and disease. Remember, the universe never loses or forgets anything or anyone, and there are rules and limits regarding behavior and refinement of the molecular structures that ARE our life. Again, think flowers and weeds, living being or fill material. I will not pretend to know any new ten commandments, but there are too many people IN AMERICA today who get away with large and small scale forms of money stealing and murder terrorism on a daily basis. We "Americans" need to fix the problems in America FIRST before creating debt (we can't pay back with ten (10) new generations of slave labor workers) to pay for the expansion of our own flawed system into another part of the world. Like duh; does anyone need to be told this? Do the books you read not support what I just said? The rest of the world that would like a piece of the American pie more than likely does not realize the fines, fees, taxes, risks, and dangers involved, which of course we won't talk about until AFTER we get that initial gigantic investment. "Some people" are ready, willing, and proud to put everybody in a world war over "their" salaries, benefits, and beliefs; who could they be? The people who get their salaries and benefits from you and me, taxes we pay, another hero government employee.

No doubt ladies and gentlemen, when you are a loud and proud shallow thinking competitive American and you make your living from creating taxes, fines, fees, war, poverty, debt, interest, and the like, you WILL seek ways to generate more fines, fees, taxes, interest, debt, poverty, etc., and convince yourself that you can get away with it again one or two more times in the next one or two years.

I believe that water, electricity, telephone, satellite communications, insurance, and a few other vital industries should be not for profit industries, and that no one on the payrolls of the companies should earn over $150,000.00 per year. If you cannot support a family of four comfortably on $150,000.00 (2009 basis), you are a poor money manager, or you are living way beyond your means, or you need a second income. I also believe that by taking advertising costs and CEO bonuses out of the cost of insurance, the cost of insurance would come down considerably. "Insurance" should be required learning in High School, at least two semesters for everyone. I know from personal experience, insurance companies will pay lawyers MORE to fight a legitimate claim than the amount of the claim. The legal world would change radically if I were allowed to directly influence the "changes" I see need improving. I have known many lawyers, most of them are creeps, some of them are super creeps. There has to be a few good ones somewhere, I just don't know where, and "good" can mean a lot of things that conflict with ethics, honesty, sobriety, fairness, and the law. Most legal work is paper work anyway, and should be taught in school to everyone, required study for all the basic needs (a trust, insurance, investments, wills, etc.), at least two semesters for every student in high school and college. America's legal system is like a 75 year old field of thorny, stinky, poisonous weeds, a home for opossum's, skunks, rats, mice, dung beetles, flies, mosquitoes, fleas, ticks, and road side trash. I am not getting into the legal system issues that need democratic attention, in my opinion, at this time. Most lawyers are liars.

Here is a serious suggestion on how to "save" the auto industry from itself, and save the consumer from the auto makers. Limit and perfect the number of engines and drive trains etc. and make all body designs interchangeable in three or four classes based on frame size; i.e. small car, mid-size, sport utility, pickup truck, etc. For example, have only twelve to fifteen engine and transmission combinations worldwide, with eighty to one hundred body style options that can be picked up and put on or off the frames. There could 1,000 or more color choices. Internationally universal filters and parts (since parts already come from around the one world economy planet), and perfect what works the best. Limit the frames and engines, improve the bodies and safety features. Only introduce new lines every five to seven years, just improve on what there is. Get rid of the seat belt law, put the cab of the vehicle in a roll cage. Give people an "ON/OFF" switch for all the stupid beepers and buzzers that tell you what you are supposed to know without being told (door ajar beeper, potentially hazardous should be optional seat belt not on beep beep beeper, etc. beeper beep). Get rid of the razor sharp edge easy to break part and fastener "war" with the car interiors and under the hood; Phillips head screws or a Philips hex head combo works better than all the "destroy to remove" cheap plastic clips in the cars in 2009. People NEED to LEARN and teach people (THEIR children) how to drive with respect. Driving with respect is superior to wearing a seat belt. Driving habits are a matter of respect, which is born from "learning." In a society that teaches pride, violence, denial, porno, religion, and drunkenness; we are pretty fortunate there are not more blood stains along the highway. If the entire world drove the same "mass produced" vehicles (specialty super cars still allowed of course), perhaps we could solve a few or even several problems at the same time. How many electrical generators could a three cylinder air driven engine "max out," how many miles or acres of electric service coverage is that at what output? Compared to a "subdivision" having its own windmill and walls of solar panels? What are we waiting for? People with the money needed to "set up shop?" Yes. Despite all the talk, it is NOT easy to get a "government grant" to start a business that plans to compete with a network of utility conglomerate lobbyists.

Cleaning up our planet and installing new electric source equipment, wow, what great employment areas. Every area should have a wind generator and solar panel wall, for emergencies and for everyday use. Many homes could have private, highly efficient, fair cost windmills (current costs for such devices are ridiculously high ((greedy)) in my opinion). We can work this out fairly, the giants in the current industry need to be controlled so they do not "take over" what they could have invented a long time ago and never share the benefits (daily) with the consumers. Cut excessive bonuses, salaries, and other waste, and see power costs come down. Again, wind and solar appear to be a great option for now.

Adding to the details of a previous subject, there is a new American plan in the works that suggests an outline for a system in which ALL citizens be trained and certified in at least three unrelated skilled areas and or specialized fields of income production, and that 100% employment is always the number one goal of our economy. One of the three jobs has to contain at least some physical labor, such as road work, home construction, landscaping, and one area of work is white collar, the third is optional. The point here is all people be trained to perform diversified job tasks or skills. All citizens will have a three "section" year, as in, for example, Period 1: seven months of full time work, 45 hours per week five days a week; Period 2: three months of continued and advanced job training, or on the job training for a transition job, or further formal education, 36 hours per week; Period 3: two months of vacation. All workers out of high school have the same program until age 55 (unless they excel and can retire earlier) when everything changes for the better. If a person is not ready for retirement but wants to work a little less, two months vacation can become three, the extra month taken from job training, and may include full retirement of the labor job; a choice. Perhaps there would be a shortage of employees in major industries, which could mean the absorption of smaller companies into larger ones, or another "shift in priorities" that demand a restructuring of certain areas; for example, tobacco forever not reproduced in any large scale, home growers only use tobacco; for example. Creating jobs and having the money to pay for the work should become our focus priority (America's #1 focus) that goes hand in hand with real education.

No one should ever suffer from a lack of money. Everyone should have an individual money and debt strategist, who will be professionally managed; and a national goal will be to eliminate private bankruptcies. All the slums should be demolished, properly disposed of and recycled, and new condominiums or duplex, or private owner residences constructed in their place. Business will become a "share the wealth" operation, and people will be taught to crave knowledge, work, and co-operation in place of being mediocre, lazy, and making things that break and become trash quickly, just to make a buck. Everyone should learn "to be their own boss." Criminals and others who refuse to co-operate will be ostracized but not tortured. Every effort to rehab delinquents will be employed, and crime will eventually (hopefully) dissipate to next to nothing. When teaching replaces arresting and beating, we will be on a new path towards harmony with the universe. Having sex with every person one can is not the primary purpose of our Human body, plus such behavior can be and is very dangerous and damaging in many ways.

In a perspective relative to the size of the universe, Humans are smaller than the micron particles Humans have to magnify 125,000 times to see an outline of the particle's independent moving body. We have come a long way from carving marks into the stone walls of caves. In another real dimension of life, high speed satellite internet is child's play. My family did not evolve from gorilla's, and we were not created in the snap of a finger. In order to get out of the depths of the slurry we are in, we have to get ready, as in being prepared, so we don't get a decompression disability by ascending to quickly from the deep.

For clarity, now consider this: "how does a person with a name like Muhamed Akbar al Sheik Ali bin Bushba ever get into a place like America, accumulate enough hair care products to blow up a skyscraper or two in a plan to kill thousands of Americans, and not get caught until acting suspicious while gathering information on how to perfect the bomb?" Do I mix the acetone with the hydrogen-peroxide or the nail polish remover?" Only in America? Not anymore. The rest of the world has a problem with America. Americans have problems with America. There are some filthy slums in America, and there should be no filthy slums in any nation. With this in mind, let's consider this, what is socialism compared to capitalism when it comes to insurance? I sold insurance for a period of time in my life, in America, and I'm qualified to tell you, it is a corrupt, manipulative, lucrative business for some, a life saver for a few, and a business that badly needs reform in the area of uniformed regulation, in my professional opinion. We all KNOW, insurance is a corrupt business, like politics, medicine, religion, investing, banking, the car business, almost anything Human (and American).

One of the first things I learned about the insurance business from the inside was "insurance companies make the most money by not paying legitimate claims." In a democratic socialist society, there would be no advertising by any insurance company, therefore, no advertising EXPENSE for insurance companies, which would free up billions of dollars every year for paying legitimate claims. Insurance should and could be automatic from birth to life exit, and include professional annual reviews (that are required like filing a tax return), but of course the premiums have to be paid, like taxes; both of which "businesses" are corrupt from a fair, ethical, perspective with integrity relative to respect for life. No one would ever be over or under insured, or overcharged. Get caught cheating an insurance company, look out and think twice. Insurance companies trying to cheat clients, victims, employees, etc. look out several times. Health professionals need to come under greater scrutiny. Testing for causes of illness will become more direct instead of "trying" EVERYTHING the insurance company WILL pay for first, when a simpler test is available. Simple blood tests and hair analysis are less costly than a barrage of "guess work try this" tests, and most hair and blood profiles can be done with a very small amount of blood and hair, like one small vile and one fourth of the hair from your last trim. Think of health as a matter that starts with intake. The cleaner the intake, the cleaner the system needing good health.

If an insurance company can write one million dollars of new insurance premium (and collect it) every year for 8 years, it will take in 36 million dollars in just 8 years, 88 million in 12 years. Subtract claims paid, wages, computer and office etc. expenses, and being an insurance company owner is usually a really great deal. Most good insurance companies will write over a million dollars of premium in far less than a year. Annual pay for "the top brass" in the insurance company list of liabilities would come down dramatically in a democratic socialist society, which would also free up tens of millions or hundreds of millions of dollars annually that could be used to pay legitimate claims, create and provide jobs and education. There could be one international insurance company (built in stages with offices everywhere). This COULD be an HONEST operation with a cost plus 12% profit ceiling. Everyone has to have insurance; life, accident, and health insurance (home owners, auto, etc.). Insurance can be low cost higher coverage, if not for the layers of legal capitalist icing that are built into the premiums. Strict controls beyond the current level of the same would have to be put in place for added security of the democratic socialist insurance industry. RESPECT and less stress will create an attitude environment that will reduce insurance claims (i.e. people will become more respectful, relaxed, careful drivers; thefts, vandalisms, arson, and other crimes will fade away, less economic stress usually means less crime). And just think, no more insurance company ads on the television, radio, newspapers, or in magazines. Hundreds of millions saved industry wide for policy holders, insurance rates reduced perhaps 35-40%, coverage increased 20%? We shall see. Again, all insurance would become automatic in a democratic socialist system, one plan fits everyone, individually. Every policy would be tailor made for every individual, no exclusions of any kind. "Demerits" would be enforced for hazardous lifestyles. All insurance would be in one individualized package for everyone; i.e. health, life, dental, property, liability, etc. Insurance becomes mandatory and adjusts with age and established insurance company tables and statistics. Advertising cost, federal fees, taxes, bonus benefits packages, legal staff, and 5th avenue offices make insurance rates go up. The price of insurance must come down. Everyone needs full coverage insurance, not a "what if coverage" insurance program. Medical professionals milk the insurance policies of all available benefits if they can, whether the "tests" are really needed or not.

Insurance is a socialist program by nature, as in everyone pitch in to help everyone, like social security. Capitalists are self money motivated, not peaceful society development motivated. War drives economies. I believe insurance should be socialized. Actuarial costs (including payroll) plus 12% is all the insurance industry can make in the way of net profit, and never less than 12%, except by a vote of the majority of the people. Everyone in the insurance industry should make a fair and good wage. By eliminating all the hype, stupid commercials, and excess everything, life will naturally improve in quality for the great majority of us. Everyone must carry their own weight in every situation without whining and crying. Everyone "has to face GOD alone" like Jesus did. I am not a Jesus freak, but he is a good example.

Another area that should be socialized is the energy production industry. Energy should be next to being free, like sunlight, water, the Earth, fire, and wind. Like in every industry, everyone should be paid a good wage. Fairness becomes an issue when some few make many millions and a large mass who made it possible for the few to make millions only receive tens of thousands. We used to call this a form of slavery. There are perhaps millions of jobs on the horizon in the old (new) environmentally friendly energy switchover industry. Where is a new Tesla? Where are the devices Tesla engineered decades ago? (Other than the Niagara Falls hydroelectric system?) If just the insurance industry and energy production industries were "democratically socialized," consumers would pay billions less every year for both and get the same or better service. Then comes the phone companies, all the different phone company signals, phones, and programs, and commercials, etc. All we need is one phone company, with five to seven different phones that do everything a phone can do with small variances between models.

In addition to what has been said about medical care, the best medical care is self managed daily care. No need to become obsessive and compulsive, but eating dead animal flesh is one of the most destructive things people can do to themselves. So is drinking too much alcohol, soda, coffee, water, eating junk food, too much sugar, and out of whack carbohydrate, sodium, protein, etc. combos. Dairy products make millions of people sick every year. Many people are unaware of their allergy to dairy products. Cow mucous by-products were never really meant for Human consumption. Stress is a huge problem on many levels. Smoking is dangerous, but marijuana should be legal, and cooked with instead of being smoked, but free will should be respected. There are over 3,500 industrial uses for hemp. Research shows that a "pot head" is less of a threat than a drunk; but neither are good examples for innocent children. Al Kida does not smoke or drink except on a *very* rare occasion, and then only very lightly and in the company of a very few persons (long time friends from childhood times).

The majority of the people in America are SLAVES to "the system" that supports government employees" regardless of skin color, gender, political party affiliation, religion, or whatever. America is a semi-socialist nation NOW. It seems to me that "our job" should be 1. secure a financial future with good planning and discipline for ourselves and family; 2. Once 1. is established, devote the rest of our lives to helping others achieve fulfillment in life; fulfillment being a spiritual position, not an economic one, and there should be no such thing as a person in a rich spiritual position who is totally lost in their personal economic situation. Work has spiritual value. Helping the less fortunate is a good karma maker, I hope (who knows what GOD thinks, we are stupid); we can't think like GOD, the brain wave energy level is too hot to handle. So when you start to tremble uncontrollably, know we can feel the presence of the Creator of the universe (where we exist temporarily, close to a gateway to other dimensions of life).

Ladies and Gentlemen, please forgive me if you think this ending is too abrupt. I say the evidence is already in, this is the closing argument that I hope opens your mind to the seriousness of controlling the government in a TRULY democratic manner. I work with and am a good friend of the people at the following web address. Please contact me through joe@ freijeworld.com; he will contact me, we're neighbors also. Please see Joe's site and buy his books, he taught me how to do a lot of things, like think clearly, and how to write. I owe him a lot, but can't seem to teach him advanced algebra; but he doesn't need it. Please also see http://www.the 7thfire.com/politics%20

www.freijeworld.com "**Deep Thoughts on the Surface**" by Paul Fletcher, Chief Bear Claw, Big Ugly Mean Guy, and Joseph P. Freije; which is currently **only** available as an e-book through **www.freijeworld.com (listen to the music)**

"Deep Thoughts on the Surface" has many color graphics that make the cost to produce such a book very costly. As an e-book however, you get a lot (a great deal) for a little in this case; a lot of entertainment, and education in a fun format.

Best Regards, and Thank You 10,000 times
Al Kida

AMERICAN FREEDOM OR FREEDUMB
DEMOCRACY SOCIALISM RELIGION GENDER GOD,
SKIN COLOR HEALTH CARE TWO PARTY POLITICS
LIFE DEATH FEAR HATE LOVE GREED DENIAL BIAS

Nothing scares Al Kida!!!!!